ESSENTIAL MUSIC THEORY
for electric

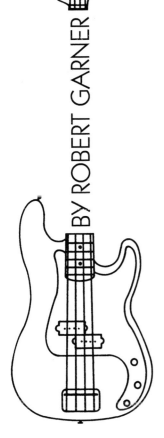

BY ROBERT GARNER

1 2 3 4 5 6 7 8 9 0

Visit us on the Web at www.melbay.com — E-mail us at email@melbay.com

Contents

Introduction

This book is designed to help guide a beginning music theory dialogue between instructor and student in private one-on-one lessons. Six areas of beginning music theory are covered: The major scale, the natural minor scale, intervals, triads, seventh chords, and harmonized major and minor scales. Fingerings, intervallic structures, and note names are also diagrammed in each chapter.

It is highly recommended that this book is used in the course of study with a professional bass instructor, though many players have found the book to be useful in self-study. A good bass teacher will help explain and demonstrate theory concepts in a live setting, and also shed additional light in terms of alternate fingerings, ear training, and gaining full technical mastery of theory concepts across the entire fingerboard.

Review worksheets are provided at the end of each chapter to ensure understanding of concepts from lesson to lesson, and answer keys are found in the back of the book.

We hope you have fun with the book, and find it useful in gaining deeper insight into the fundamentals of music theory for electric bass.

Diagram of Page Layout

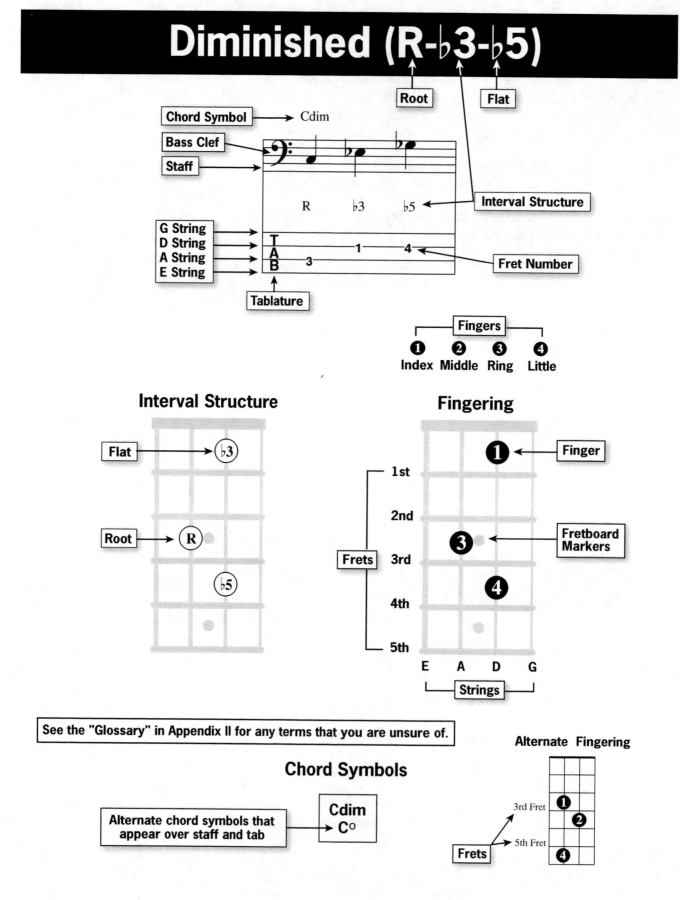

See the "Glossary" in Appendix II for any terms that you are unsure of.

The notes shown on this staff diagram begin with the low open E string, and ascend to the twelfth fret G on the G string. All of the remaining notes require a sharp (♯) or a flat (♭) to be placed in front of the desired note. For example, you can call the 2nd fret E string note an F♯ or G♭.

The A on the fifth fret of the E string is the same as the open A string. They are both notated with the same A on the staff (the lowest space on the staff). Keep in mind that one note on the staff may be represented by several different notes on the fret board.

Accidentals - sharps (♯), double-sharps (✗) flats (♭), double-flats (♭♭) and natural signs (♮) that appear next to notes on the staff.

♭ = flat, lower note 1/2 step (1 fret)

♭♭ = double flat, lower note whole step (2 frets)

♯ = sharp, raise note 1/2 step (1 fret)

✗ = double sharp, raise note whole step (2 frets)

♮ = natural, return note to it's original place

Notes of the Neck

Note Names – Sharps

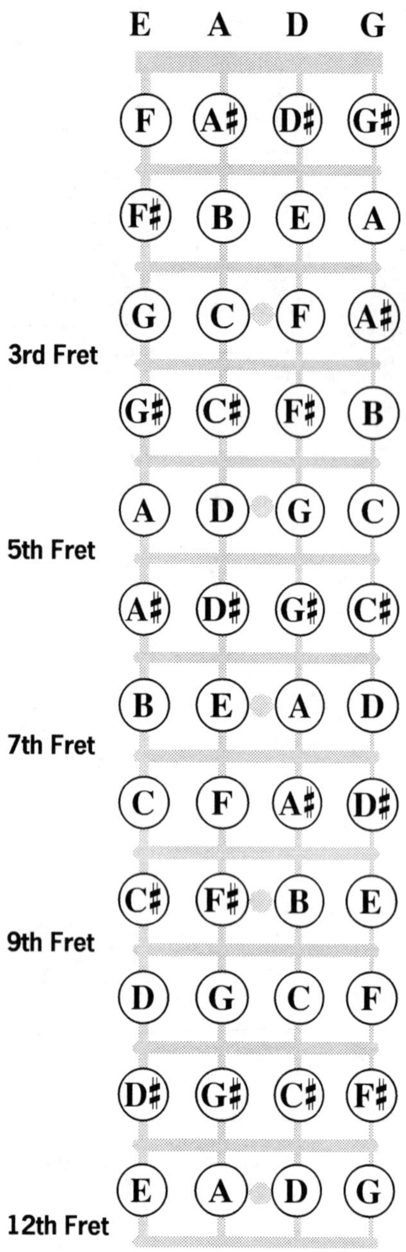

E	A	D	G
F	A#	D#	G#
F#	B	E	A
G	C	F	A#

3rd Fret

G#	C#	F#	B
A	D	G	C

5th Fret

A#	D#	G#	C#
B	E	A	D

7th Fret

C	F	A#	D#
C#	F#	B	E

9th Fret

D	G	C	F
D#	G#	C#	F#
E	A	D	G

12th Fret

Note Names – Flats

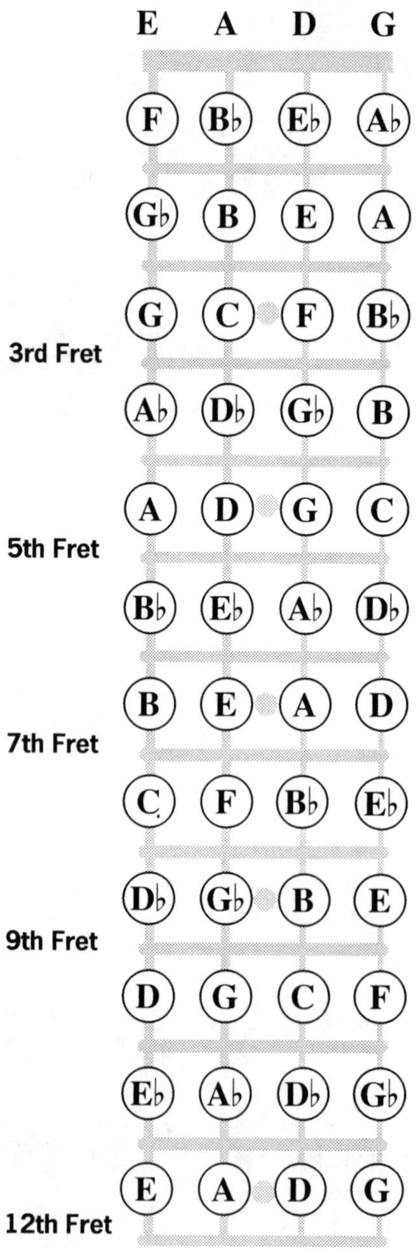

E	A	D	G
F	Bb	Eb	Ab
Gb	B	E	A
G	C	F	Bb

3rd Fret

Ab	Db	Gb	B
A	D	G	C

5th Fret

Bb	Eb	Ab	Db
B	E	A	D

7th Fret

C	F	Bb	Eb
Db	Gb	B	E

9th Fret

D	G	C	F
Eb	Ab	Db	Gb
E	A	D	G

12th Fret

Shown above are the notes of the neck up to the 12th fret. Notes shown with two names (ex. A#/Bb) are called "enharmonic" notes. This means that they can be called two different names, but sound the same. The notes beginning with the 12th fret (E-A-D-G) are the same as the open strings (the open string notes EADG appear again at the 12th fret and are one octave higher than their open string counterparts of the same name). From this point, all of the notes are repeated one octave higher (ex. E string - 12th fret same note as open E; 13th fret same note as 1st fret F; 14th fret F#/Gb same note as 2nd fret etc.).

6

Tuning

1. Using Fretted Notes

5th Fret

2. Using Harmonics

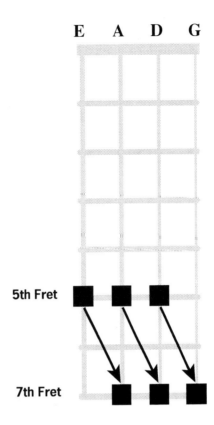

5th Fret

7th Fret

Tuning is a basic requirement for playing any stringed instrument. Practice the two methods shown below, but use an electronic tuner when available.

1. Tuning with Fretted Notes – Tune your low open E string to a piano or pitch pipe. Next, place your fretting hand first finger on the 5th fret A (on the E string). As this note rings out, play the open A string and try to match the two notes. Turn the A string tuning key until the notes match exactly. Repeat the process on the next two strings. If a string is even slightly out of tune in any place it may alter the entire tuning sequence, so tune carefully.

2. Tuning with Harmonics – Tune the open E string to a piano, or pitch pipe. Next, place your fretting hand first finger on the fifth fret A (on the E string), **but do not press all the way down - finger is placed above the metal not in the actual fret space.** Your fretting hand finger should be directly on top of the string at the fifth fret of the E string. When the note is plucked with your right hand, an artificial note called a **harmonic** will ring out. Match this harmonic with the harmonic on the seventh fret of the A string. If played correctly, you should be able to remove your hand from the string and turn the tuning keys while the notes continue to ring out. Repeat the process on the A, D, and G strings.

Cycle of Fifths

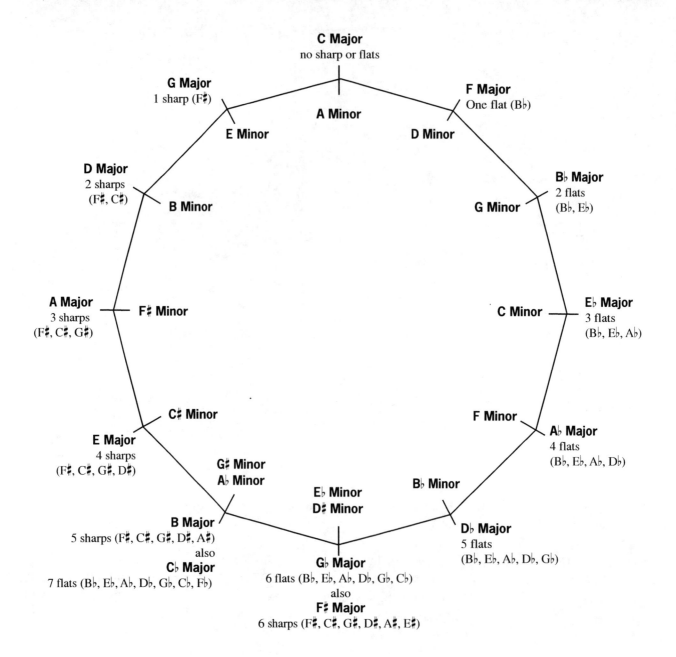

Cycle of Fifths — Key Signatures

This chart shows key signatures for major and minor scales. This chart is also commonly referred to as "the circle of fifths" or "the circle of fourths."

Chapter One
Major Scale

The major scale is the fundamental scale representing major tonality. When a **key signature** (see pg.13) is presented on the staff, it fundamentally refers to this scale or tonality (or its minor scale, see pg. 19)

The major scale is presented here in **one octave form** (see pg. 11, "Interval Structure"). Understanding this one octave scale form will highlight the function of the scale when it is applied to the full range of the neck. Examples in this chapter are designed to give you a grasp on **interval structure, fingerings, note names,** and **key signatures**. All examples are played on the root C, but when you move the pattern to any other root note, you will automatically be able to play that scale. Combine the 12 different notes on the neck with the major scale pattern, and you will then know 12 scales. Practice major scale patterns in all 12 keys, but also memorize the note names, staff notation, and interval relationships.

At the top of each page is the standard music notation for the scale, with tablature underneath it. In the left column is a vertical graph of the interval structure, and the right column shows the fingering.

As a beginning or intermediate player, playing scales can be an opportunity to develop technique and sound. Practice the C scale ascending and descending very slowly, focusing on long connected notes. Avoid playing short, staccato notes at first. Also avoid "drag shifting" (playing each note with the first or fourth finger), and use the fingerings exactly as they are written here. Notice that the fingering shown for this scale will enable you to play it without shifting your hand up or down the neck. For example (see following page), in 2nd position C Major (1st finger on the 2nd fret), the left-hand first finger covers all the notes on the second fret, the second finger on the third fret, the third finger on the fourth fret, and the fourth finger on the fifth fret. If you start to shift your fingers up or down the neck in order to play this one octave scale, then stop and review the correct fingering.

Remember that learning this one octave pattern highlights the interval structure of a scale. When you fully understand this structure, practice the scale on the full range of your bass. A C major scale contains the notes **C-D-E-F-G-A-B-C**, so you should be able to play every one of those notes anywhere they appear on the neck.

Major Scale

Interval Structure

See following page for more on "Interval Structure"

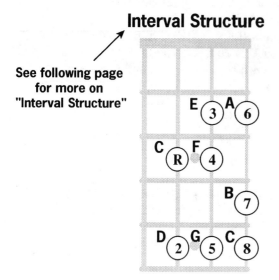

Fingering

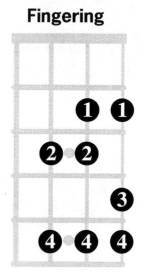

The major scale shown here is in one octave form so that you may gain a thorough understanding of its structure. Don't limit scales to just the notes in this octave. Now that you understand the note structure, begin to play the scale notes all over the neck. If a C major scale is composed of the notes **C-D-E-F-G-A-B-C**, then every one of those notes on your neck is part of the scale.

Alternate Fingering

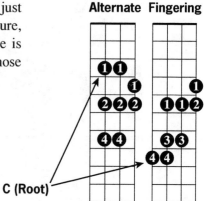

C (Root)

10

The Whole Step- Half Step Relationship

Another helpful guide to understanding scales is the whole-half step relationship. A **whole step** is equal to two frets distance between two notes, and a **half-step** is equal to one fret between two notes. Shown below is the whole-half step sequence for all of the major scales. This is a sequence that should be memorized:

Whole - Whole - Half - Whole - Whole - Whole - Half

R-2   2-3   3-4   4-5   5-6   6-7   7-8

Another easy way to remember this formula is to know where the half-steps occur. In any major scale, the half-steps occur between the 3rd and 4th, and 7th and root.

Interval Structure – Major Scales

If you count notes as you ascend up the scale, you will see that C-D-E-F-G-A-B-C is equal to R-2-3-4-5-6-7-8. **The term interval specifically refers to a distance between the root, and any number within the scale** (ex. Root-2, Root-7, Root-5, etc.). Though the first note of the scale may be called the 'one', it is most commonly called the root.

When learning intervals in ascending order (as shown in the first diagram of the previous page), be aware of descending intervals as well. Whether an interval is descending or ascending, it is still considered an interval.

Shown below are the more specific names for each interval in a major scale. Memorize this sequence. A more detailed discussion is presented in Chapter 3.

This chart corresponds with the "Interval Structure" chart shown on page 10.

1. **Root (R)**

2. **Major Second (2)**

3. **Major Third (3)**

4. **Perfect Fourth (4)**

5. **Perfect Fifth (5)**

6. **Major Sixth (6)**

7. **Major Seventh (7)**

8. **Octave (8)**

Examples of Intervals

1. The notes **'C' and 'A'** are called a **major sixth (R-6).**

2. The notes **'C' and 'G'** are called a **perfect fifth (R-5).**

3. The notes **'C' and 'D'** are called a **major second (R-2).**

The Musical Alphabet- Understanding Intervals, Scales, and Chords

If note spelling seems like a daunting task, consider this: The English alphabet that we use to spell thousands of words has 26 letters. The musical alphabet has only seven:

A B C D E F G

The first step to knowing correct interval, chord, and scale note spelling requires you to recite the musical alphabet from any given letter. For example:

The alphabet from A-A: A B C D E F G A
from B-B: B C D E F G A B
from C-C: C D E F G A B C
from D-D: D E F G A B C D
from E-E: E F G A B C D E
from F- F: F G A B C D E F
from G-G: G A B C D E F G

> **Important**
> Don't confuse these notes with the major or minor scales. They are simply sequences of letters that will aid alphabetical spelling.

You can also visualize the alphabet in this way:

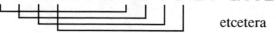

A B C D E F G A B C D E F G A B C D E F G A B C D E F G

etcetera

An example to illustrate how correct scale spelling works. There are seven different notes in any of the major or minor scales, and there are seven different letters in the musical alphabet. Major and minor scales should have one of each letter represented. The first example is the G major scale:

G-A-B-C-D-E-F♯

One of each letter of the musical alphabet is represented. If the F♯ had been called G♭, then the scale would have had two kinds of G's.

Now try D♭ major:

D♭-E♭-F-G♭-A♭-B♭-C

Notice that there are more accidentals in this example, but each letter of the musical alphabet is represented.

Here is an example of a C♯ major scale:

C♯-D♯-E♯-F♯-G♯-A♯-B♯

All of the notes in C♯ major sound the same as D♭ major, but each letter has a different name. The seven letters of the musical alphabet are also represented in this C♯ Major Scale. As a general rule, each scale will contain either **all sharps** or **all flats** for accidentals, but not both. If you have written out a major or natural minor scale and you see a combination of sharps and flats, at least one letter of the musical alphabet has been left out. Here is an example of the wrong way to write a scale:

Wrong way to write a scale: A-B-C♯-D-E-G̶♭-G♯

This series of notes will sound like a correct A major scale, but there are two kinds of G represented, and no trace of the letter F. The correct spelling should include F♯ instead of G♭.

Key Signatures

For every major scale, there is a key signature that should appear at the beginning of the staff. This minimizes the number of accidentals to be written on the page because they are already assumed to be there. For example, the key of D major contains the notes D-E-F#-G-A-B-C#. The key signature for this scale places the accidental signs (2 sharps) at the beginning of the staff on the second space (C), and the 4th line (F). This means that every F and C written on the staff (at any octave) should automatically be sharped.

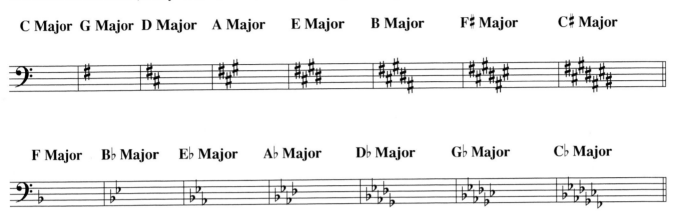

For more on key signatures, see the "Cycle of Fifths" chart in the Introduction.

Table of Major Scales

12 Major Scales

R = Root
2 = Major Second
3 = Major Third
4 = Perfect Fourth
5 = Perfect Fifth
6 = Major Sixth
7 = Major Seventh
8 = Octave

	R	2	3	4	5	6	7	8
1	C	D	E	F	G	A	B	C
2	F	G	A	B♭	C	D	E	F
3	B♭	C	D	E♭	F	G	A	B♭
4	E♭	F	G	A♭	B♭	C	D	E♭
5	A♭	B♭	C	D♭	E♭	F	G	A♭
6	D♭	E♭	F	G♭	A♭	B♭	C	D♭
7	F♯	G♯	A♯	B	C♯	D♯	E♯	F♯
8	B	C♯	D♯	E	F♯	G♯	A♯	B
9	E	F♯	G♯	A	B	C♯	D♯	E
10	A	B	C♯	D	E	F♯	G♯	A
11	D	E	F♯	G	A	B	C♯	D
12	G	A	B	C	D	E	F♯	G

The roots of the scales are highlighted in bold, and are shown in the first vertical column. The remaining notes of each scale proceed in the horizontal row. The top vertical row displays the standard interval structure of all major scales and corresponds with the scale notes listed below them.

Review Questions

I.

1. Find the root of the major scale that contains the notes **G, F, C, A, E, B,** and **D**. Hint: compare the accidentals for each scale with the scales in the "Table of Major Scales" chart on page 13.

2. Find the root of the major scale that contains the notes **B♭, D, F, C, G, A,** and **E♭**.

3. Find the root of the major scale that contains the notes **E♭, D♭, G, A♭, C, B♭,** and **F**.

4. Find the root of the major scale that contains the notes **B, E, C♯, G, A, D,** and **F♯**.

5. Find the root of the major scale that contains the notes **G♯, B, C♯, F♯, A, E, and D**.

6. Name two major scales that contain the notes **B♭.** and **D♭** (both notes in the same scale).

7. Name two major scales that contain the notes **A♭** and **D♭** (both notes in the same scale).

8. The sixth note of a D major scale is _____.

9. The fourth note of a B major scale is _____.

10. The third note of a B♭ major scale is _____.

11. **C** is the fifth note of the _____ major scale.

12. **A♭** is the second note of a _____ major scale.

13. The seventh note of a G major scale is _____.

14. The _____ major scale has five flats in the key signature.

15. Name the three notes that are flatted in an E♭ major scale _____, _____, _____.

16. The _____ major scale has two flats in the key signature.

17. **G** is the fourth note of the _____ major scale.

18. Name the intervals of a major scale that are "major" in quality _____, _____, _____, and _____.

19. Name the intervals of a major scale that are "perfect" in quality.

20. Name the first four notes of an **A** major scale_____, _____, _____, and _____.

II. True or False

1. An E major scale contains two sharps in the key signature.

2. There are five sharps in a G♯ major scale.

3. To correctly spell a major scale, all seven letters of the musical alphabet should be represented.

4. The four accidentals in an E major scale are **F♯, G♯, D♯,** and **C♯**.

5. The third note of the G♭ major scale is **C♭**.

6. The six accidentals in an F♯ major scale are **F♯, G♯, A♯, B♯, C♯,** and **D♯**.

7. E major and A major have a key signature of 3 sharps.

8. There are four flats in the key of D♭ major.

9. There are two sharps in the key of D major.

10. There are three flats in the key of G major.

III. Use correct alphabetical spelling to list the notes of the 12 major scales. Each letter of the alphabet should be represented. Play each one octave scale on your bass to find the notes, and use the "Notes of the Neck" chart in the introduction if needed. Avoid using the Table of Major Scales for this exercise.

1. C Major: ____ ____ ____ ____ ____ ____ ____

2. F Major: ____ ____ ____ ____ ____ ____ ____

3. B♭ Major: ____ ____ ____ ____ ____ ____ ____

4. E♭ Major: ____ ____ ____ ____ ____ ____ ____

5. A♭ Major: ____ ____ ____ ____ ____ ____ ____

6. D♭ Major: ____ ____ ____ ____ ____ ____ ____

7. G♭ Major: ____ ____ ____ ____ ____ ____ ____

8. B Major: ____ ____ ____ ____ ____ ____ ____

9. E Major: ____ ____ ____ ____ ____ ____ ____

10. A Major: ____ ____ ____ ____ ____ ____ ____

11. D Major: ____ ____ ____ ____ ____ ____ ____

12. G Major: ____ ____ ____ ____ ____ ____ ____

IV. Label the notes of each scale on the entire range of the fretboards shown. Use correct note spelling.

Example

C Major

E	A	D	G
F			
	B	E	A
G	C	F	
			B
A	D	G	C
B	E	A	D
C	F		

F Major

B♭ Major

E♭ Major

A♭ Major

D♭ Major

G♭ Major

B Major

E Major

A Major

D Major

G Major

V. Using correct notes and accidentals, label the notes of each major scale (begin with the root shown in ascending order). Use the "Notes of the Staff" chart in the introduction if needed.
Ex.

VI. Find the root of each scale shown on the staff below. The first note shown is not necessarily the root.
Ex. A♭ Major

Chapter Two
Natural Minor Scale

The minor scale represents the opposite tonality of major. Generally speaking, music is categorized into either a major or minor key. When a minor tonality is established, it is represented by a natural minor scale or related mode (see page 24). Like the major scale, the minor scale can be applied to any of the 12 different notes on the neck to play 12 more scales. Don't rely on the patterns alone, though. After the pattern is memorized, concentrate on learning the note names and interval structure.

Since scales sharing the same key signature are related, they are often referred to as **relative**. Every major scale has a relative minor key, and every minor scale has a relative major key. **To find the relative minor key, go to the major sixth interval of a major scale.** This note is the root of the relative minor key (related Natural Minor Scale). For example, the major sixth interval from the root C of a C major scale is A. Therefore, the relative minor key from C major is A minor. Both C major and A minor contain the same seven notes, but each has a different root.

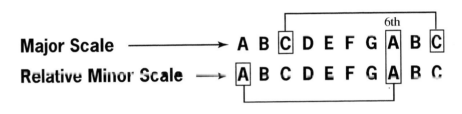

To find a relative major scale, go to the **third note** of the selected **minor scale**. If you play a major scale pattern based on that note, you will find that the related major scale contains all of the same notes as the original minor scale. This is why a key signature represents both a major and relative minor scale.

Correct alphabet spelling also applies to the minor scale. Use the same method described in Chapter One.

Also note that the minor scale shown above is based on the root A to illustrate relative minor scales. The examples shown in the chapter are shown on the root C (the relative major scale of C minor is E♭ major).

Minor Scale

Interval Structure

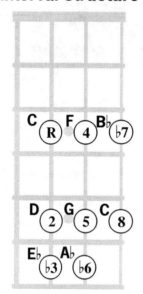

Fingering

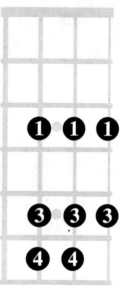

Alternate Fingering

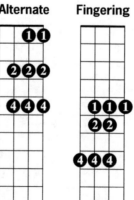

Key Signatures

Listed below are the key signatures for the natural minor scale. The related major scale of each key shares the same signature.

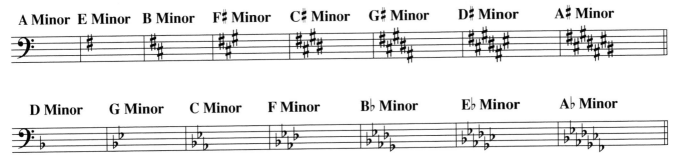

Also see the "Cycle of Fifths" table in the Introduction. R=Root

Table of Minor Scales

R	2	♭3	4	5	♭6	♭7	8
A	B	C	D	E	F	G	A
D	E	F	G	A	B♭	C	D
G	A	B♭	C	D	E♭	F	G
C	D	E♭	F	G	A♭	B♭	C
F	G	A♭	B♭	C	D♭	E♭	F
B♭	C	D♭	E♭	F	G♭	A♭	B♭
D♯	E♯	F♯	G♯	A♯	B	C♯	D♯
G♯	A♯	B	C♯	D♯	E	F♯	G♯
C♯	D♯	E	F♯	G♯	A	B	C♯
F♯	G♯	A	B	C♯	D	E	F♯
B	C♯	D	E	F♯	G	A	B
E	F♯	G	A	B	C	D	E

R = Root
2 = Major Second
♭3 = Minor Third
4 = Perfect Fourth
5 = Perfect Fifth
♭6 = Minor Sixth
♭7 = Minor Seventh
8 = Octave

Shifting Technique for Major and Minor Scales

When you begin to play scales outside of the one octave pattern, a shifting problem often occurs. A common beginning tendency is to employ a jagged one finger shifting pattern that will impede the flow across the strings and frets. As you begin to shift out of the first octave, play the notes of the scale within a four or five fret area of the fretboard wherever possible. This makes a smooth transition between notes, and will immediately begin to clean up your overall sound.

When playing major and minor scales, there are six finger patterns that can be applied. Though you may use others that are not listed here, these shifting patterns will cover major and minor scales with only a few exceptions. Remember – these are only combinations of finger patterns used to play major and minor scales- don't get hung up on this section for too long. They are applied in the exercises on the following page.

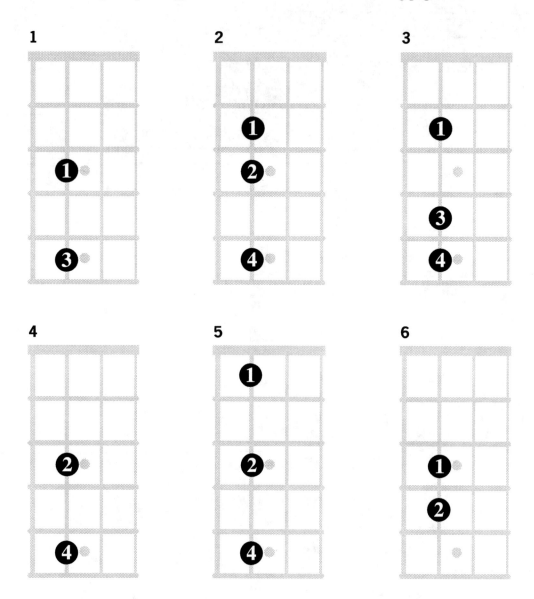

When playing ascending scales, picture the notes that you are trying to play, and group them using one of the six fingerings on the previous page. You may also use one of the blank 24 fret grids in the back of the book to label all the notes of a particular scale, then apply the fingerings where they are needed. Practice scales in ascending and descending order (for practice, use the same fingerings when going up and down the neck).

Check out these examples of a 2 octave C major scale:

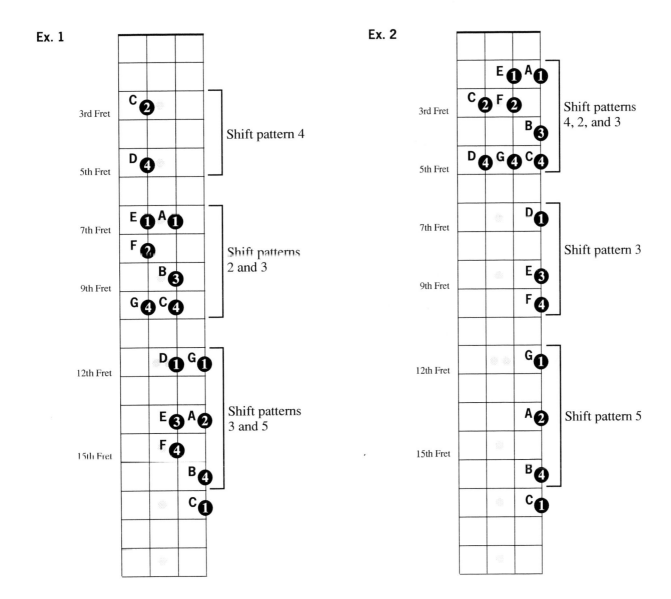

These are only two examples of extended range major scales. The finger patterns shown on the opposite page can be applied to all 24 major and minor scales (12 major, 12 minor). There are many shifting possibilities for each scale. Make it your goal to play through each major and minor scale (extended range) in all 24 keys, and play each scale at least four different ways (**four different finger shifting patterns for each scale**). Always ascend and descend the same way. The appendix contains a blank tablature grid similar to the ones shown above, with four per page. Make at least 24 copies of this sheet, and label each page with a different major or minor scale. Proceed to label all of the notes of the given scale on each of the four grids. Then use the finger patterns on page 22 to map out a logical shifting pattern for each.

Interval Structure – Minor Scales

Shown below are the specific names for each interval in a minor scale. Memorize this sequence. A more detailed discussion is presented in Chapter 3.

1. **Root (R)**
2. **Major Second (2)**
3. **Minor Third (3)**
4. **Perfect Fourth (4)**
5. **Perfect Fifth (5)**
6. **Minor Sixth (6)**
7. **Minor Seventh (7)**
8. **Octave (8)**

Examples of Intervals

1. The notes **C and A♭** are called a **minor sixth (R-♭6)**.
2. The notes **C and G** are called a **perfect fifth (R-5)**.
3. The notes **C and E♭** are called a **minor third (R-♭3)**.

Additional Minor Scales

Though only the Natural Minor scale is detailed in Chapter Two, it is important to note three other commonly used minor scales: Harmonic Minor, the Dorian Mode, and Melodic Minor. All are variations of the Natural Minor scale, and represent the minor tonality. The review section will only cover the Natural Minor scale.

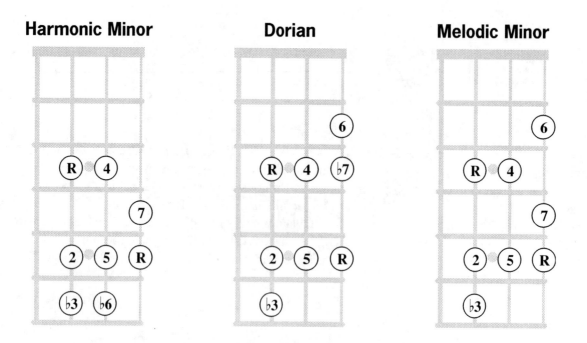

Harmonic Minor   **Dorian**   **Melodic Minor**

Review Questions

I. Short Answer

1. Find the root of the minor scale that contains the notes **G, F, C, A, E, B,** and **D**. Hint: compare the accidentals for each scale with the scales in the "Table of minor Scales" chart on page 13.

2. Find the root of the minor scale that contains the notes **B♭, D♭, F, C, G, A♭,** and **E♭**.

3. Find the root of the minor scale that contains the notes **E♭, D, G, A♭, C, B♭,** and **F**.

4. Find the root of the minor scale that contains the notes **B♭, E♭, C, G, A, D,** and **F**.

5. Find the root of the minor scale that contains the notes **G♯, B, C♯, F♯, A, E,** and **D**.

6. The relative minor scale of G major is _____.

7. The relative minor scale of E♭ major is _____.

8. If **D** is the root of the minor scale, then the relative major is _____.

9. If **A♭** is the root of the minor scale, then _____ is the relative major scale.

10. B♭ minor and _____ share the same key signature of five flats.

11. C is the fifth note of the _____ minor scale.

12. The relative minor scale of B♭ major is _____.

13. The relative major scale of F minor is _____.

14. The _____ minor scale has four flats in the key signature.

15. Name the three notes that are flatted in a C minor scale _____ _____ _____.

16. The _____ minor scale has two flats in the key signature.

17. **A** is the fourth note of the _____ minor scale.

18. Name the interval of a minor scale that is "major" in quality _____.

19. Name the intervals of a minor scale that are "perfect" in quality _____, _____.

20. Name the intervals of a minor scale that are "minor" in quality _____, _____, and _____.

II. True or False

1. The B minor scale contains two sharps in the key signature.

2. There are five sharps in a G♯ minor scale.

3. The relative minor scale of E♭ major is E♭ minor.

4. The four accidentals in a C♯ minor scale are **C♯, E♭, F♯,** and **A♭**.

5. A minor scale must always be played from the root to be considered a minor scale.

6. The relative minor scale of D major is C♯ minor.

7. The main finger pattern shown for the minor scale in chapter three does not use the second finger.

8. There are four flats in the key of F minor.

9. Every key signature represents one major and one minor scale.

10. There are three flats in the key of G minor.

III. Use correct alphabetical spelling to list the notes of each of the 12 minor scales. One of each letter of the alphabet should be represented. Play each scale on your bass, and write one note at a time (with a pencil). Use the note chart ("Notes of the Neck") in the introduction for reference. To obtain the maximum benefits of this exercise, avoid using the "Table of Minor Scales" chart.

1. C Minor: ____ ____ ____ ____ ____ ____ ____

2. F Minor: ____ ____ ____ ____ ____ ____ ____

3. B♭ Minor: ____ ____ ____ ____ ____ ____ ____

4. E♭ Minor: ____ ____ ____ ____ ____ ____ ____

5. G♯ Minor: ____ ____ ____ ____ ____ ____ ____

6. C♯ Minor: ____ ____ ____ ____ ____ ____ ____

7. F♯ Minor: ____ ____ ____ ____ ____ ____ ____

8. B Minor: ____ ____ ____ ____ ____ ____ ____

9. E Minor: ____ ____ ____ ____ ____ ____ ____

10. A Minor: ____ ____ ____ ____ ____ ____ ____

11. D Minor: ____ ____ ____ ____ ____ ____ ____

12. G Minor: ____ ____ ____ ____ ____ ____ ____

IV. Label the notes of each scale on the entire range of the fretboards shown. Use correct note spelling. This is similar to the exercise on page 16.

C minor

F minor

B♭ minor

E♭ minor

G♯ minor

C♯ minor

F♯ minor

B minor

E minor

A minor

D minor

G minor

V. Write the notes of each minor scale in ascending order on the staff, starting with the given root. Use the "Notes Of The Staff" chart in the introduction if needed.

VI. Name each minor scale shown on the staff below.

Chapter Three
Intervals

The term **interval** refers to the distance between two notes. Intervals are essential to understanding chord structures, scales, and root movements of chords.

Each page highlights several different possibilities of understanding a particular interval. **All fretboard diagrams depict intervals from the root note C**, so once you have memorized an interval you should immediately apply it to **different roots**. For example, a minor second is any set of two notes spaced a fret apart. Move the example for the root C (C-Db) to the root A. The minor second interval from root A is Bb, which is also a fret apart. Therefore, any two notes that are a fret apart from each other can be referred to as a minor second.

Also shown is the root-interval structure (ex. R-b2 on the following page) in the left vertical diagram, and a fingering in the right vertical diagram (there may more than one). Standard music notation is displayed at the top of the page, with bass tab below it. At the bottom of each page, there is a table of 12 possible interval relationships with their note names. In the top column of the table the root is shown, and the interval is written below. Each interval is also described by its sum of whole and half steps. A **half step** is equal to one fret, a **whole step** is equal to two frets. Other symbols used to describe intervals and notes are **sharps** (♯), which means to raise a note by one fret (ex. C♯); **double sharps** (✗), means to raise a note by two frets (ex. G✗); **flats** (♭) means to lower a note by one fret (ex. Db); **double flats** (♭♭), means to lower a note by two frets (ex. B♭♭); and **naturals** (♮) means to return a note to its original position (ex. C♮).

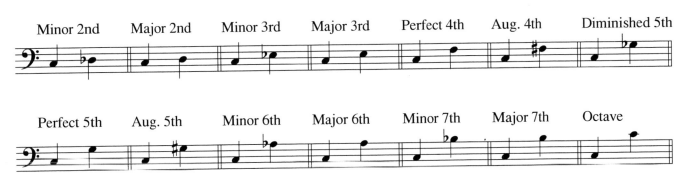

The fingerings in this chapter should be used as a guide. There are several possible correct fingerings for each example, but only one will be given.

Minor Second (R-♭2)

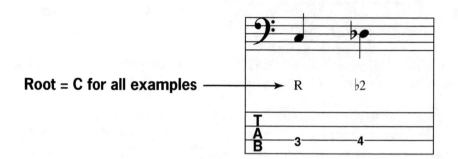

Root = C for all examples ⟶ R   ♭2

Interval Structure   ## Fingering

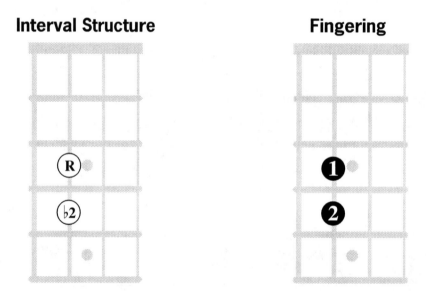

A minor second is equal to a **half step**, or one fret distance between two notes. In addition to structure and fingering, memorize the sound as well.

When the patterns are moved to different roots, the following minor seconds are generated:

Root	C	C♯	D	D♯	E	F	F♯	G	G♯	A	A♯	B
Minor 2nd	D♭	D	E♭	E	F	G♭	G	A♭	A	B♭	B	C

Major Second (R-2)

Interval Structure

Fingering

Root = C for
all examples →

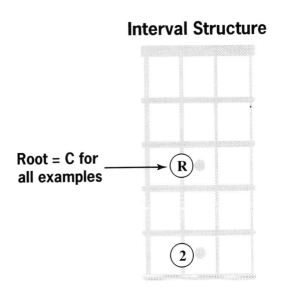

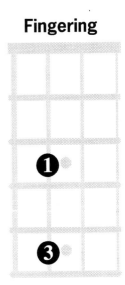

A major second is equal to one **whole step**, or two frets distance apart. This interval is the second note of a major and minor scale.

When the patterns are moved to different roots, the following major seconds are generated:

Root	C	C#	D	Eb	E	F	F#	G	Ab	A	Bb	B
Major 2nd	D	D#	E	F	F#	G	G#	A	Bb	B	C	C#

If you need extra help applying this information to your fretboard, refer to the "Notes of the Neck" chart in the introduction.

Minor Third (R-♭3)

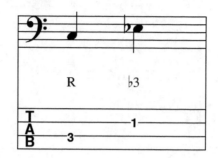

Interval Structure

Fingering

Root = C for all examples

A minor third interval is equal to one and a half steps, or three frets distance apart. This interval is the third note of a natural minor scale.

When the patterns are moved to different roots, the following minor thirds are generated:

Root	C	C♯	D	D♯	E	F	F♯	G	G♯	A	B♭	B
Minor 3rd	E♭	E	F	F♯	G	A♭	A	B♭	B	C	D♭	D

Major Third (R-3)

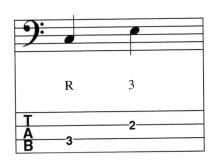

Interval Structure

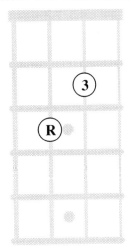

Fingering

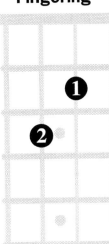

A major third is equal to two whole steps, or four frets distance apart. This interval is the third note of a major scale.

When the patterns are moved to different roots, the following major thirds are generated:

Root	C	Db	D	Eb	E	F	F#	G	Ab	A	Bb	B
Major 3rd	E	F	F#	G	G#	A	A#	B	C	C#	D	D#

Perfect Fourth (R-4)

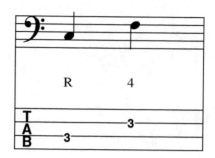

Interval Structure

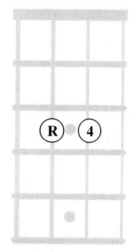

Fingering

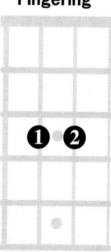

There are two and a half steps in a perfect fourth, or five frets distance apart.

When the patterns are moved to different roots, the following perfect fourths are generated:

Root	C	C♯	D	D♯	E	F	F♯	G	A♭	A	B♭	B
Perfect 4th	F	F♯	G	G♯	A	B♭	B	C	D♭	D	E♭	E

Augmented Fourth (R-♯4)

Interval Structure

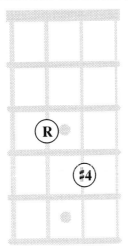

Fingering

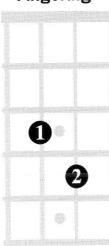

An augmented fourth is equal to three whole steps, or six frets distance apart. This interval is also called a **tritone**, and it divides an octave equally into two parts.

When the patterns are moved to different roots, the following augmented fourths are generated:

Root	C	D♭	D	E♭	E	F	F♯	G	A♭	A	B♭	B
Aug. 4th	F♯	G	G♯	A	A♯	B	B♯	C♯	D	D♯	E	E♯

Diminished Fifth (R-♭5)

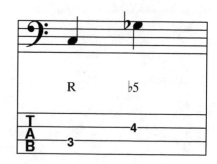

Interval Structure	**Fingering**

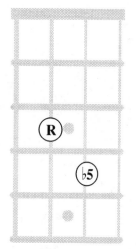

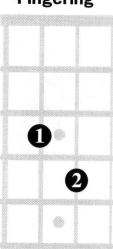

A diminished fifth is equal to three whole steps, or six frets distance apart. It may also be called a **tritone,** and it divides the octave equally in half. This interval sounds the same as an augmented fourth.

When the patterns are moved to different roots, the following diminished fifths are generated:

Root	C	C#	D	D#	E	F	F#	G	G#	A	B♭	B
Dim. 5th	G♭	G	A♭	A	B♭	C♭	C	D♭	D	E♭	F♭	F

Perfect Fifth (R-5)

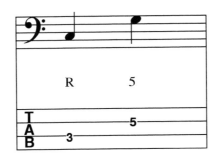

Interval Structure

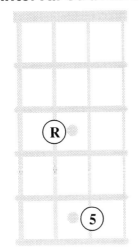

Fingering

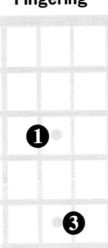

A perfect fifth is equal to three and a half steps, and the notes are seven frets apart. This interval is the fifth note of a major and minor scale.

When the patterns are moved to different roots, the following perfect fifths are generated:

Root	C	C♯	D	E♭	E	F	F♯	G	A♭	A	B♭	B
Perfect 5th	G	G♯	A	B♭	B	C	C♯	D	E♭	E	F	F♯

Augmented Fifth (R-♯5)

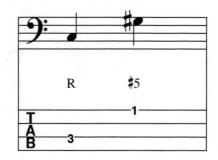

Interval Structure	Fingering
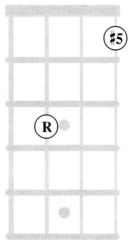	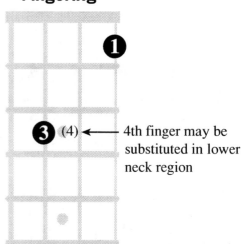

4th finger may be substituted in lower neck region

An augmented fifth is equal to four whole steps, or eight frets between two notes. This interval also sounds the same as a minor sixth.

When the patterns are moved to different roots, the following augmented fifths are generated:

Root	C	C♯	D	E♭	E	F	F♯	G	A♭	A	B♭	B
Aug. 5th	G♯	G𝄪	A♯	B	B♯	C♯	C𝄪	D♯	E	E♯	F♯	F𝄪

Minor Sixth (R-♭6)

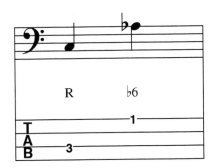

Interval Structure

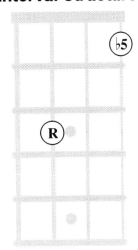

Fingering

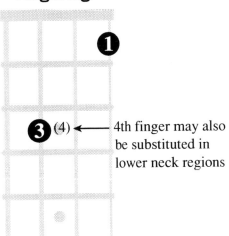

4th finger may also be substituted in lower neck regions

A minor sixth is equal to four whole steps, and has eight frets distance between two notes. It also sounds the same as an augmented fifth, and is the sixth note of a minor scale.

When the patterns are moved to different roots, the following minor sixths are generated:

Root	C	C♯	D	D♯	E	F	F♯	G	G♯	A	B♭	B
Minor 6th	A♭	A	B♭	B	C	D♭	D	E♭	E	F	G♭	G

39

Major Sixth (R-6)

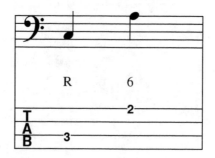

Interval Structure

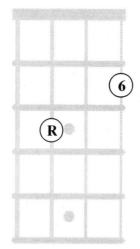

Fingering

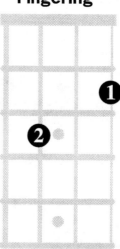

A major sixth is equal to four and a half steps, or nine frets distance between two notes. The major sixth is the sixth note of a major scale.

When the patterns are moved to different roots, the following major sixths are generated:

Root	C	Db	D	Eb	E	F	F#	G	Ab	A	Bb	B
Major 6th	A	Bb	B	C	C#	D	D#	E	F	F#	G	G#

40

Minor Seventh (R-♭7)

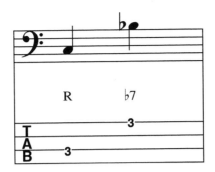

Interval Structure

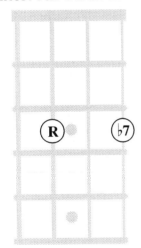

Fingering

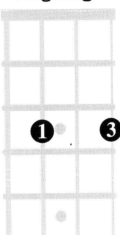

A minor seventh is equal to five whole steps, or ten frets distance between two notes. This interval is the seventh note of a minor scale.

When the patterns are moved to different roots, the following minor sevenths are generated:

Root	C	C♯	D	E♭	E	F	F♯	G	A♭	A	B♭	B
Minor 7th	B♭	B	C	D♭	D	E♭	E	F	G♭	G	A♭	A

Major Seventh (R-7)

Interval Structure

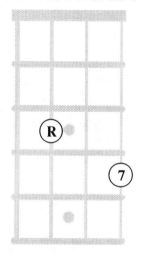

Fingering

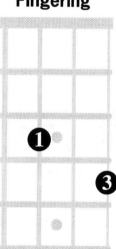

A major seventh is equal to five and a half steps, or eleven frets distance between two notes. This interval is the seventh note of the major scale.

When the patterns are moved to different roots, the following major sevenths are generated:

Root	C	D♭	D	E♭	E	F	F♯	G	A♭	A	B♭	B
Major 7th	B	C	C♯	D	D♯	E	E♯	F♯	G	G♯	A	A♯

Octave (R-8)

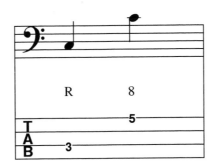

Interval Structure

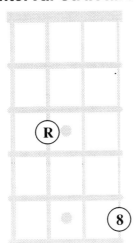

Fingering

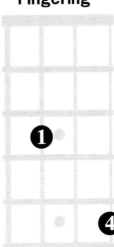

An octave is equal to six whole steps, or twelve frets distance between two notes. It is the eighth note of a major and minor scale.

When the patterns are moved to different roots, the following octaves are generated:

Root	C	C♯	D	E♭	E	F	F♯	G	G♯	A	B♭	B
Octave	C	C♯	D	E♭	E	F	F♯	G	G♯	A	B♭	B

43

Linear Intervals

Root = C

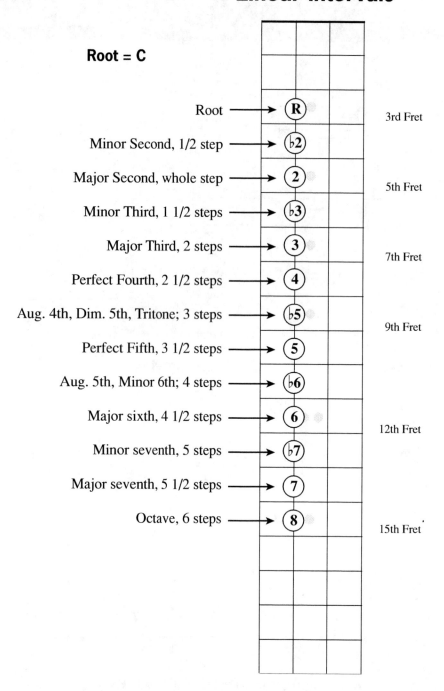

Root → (R)   3rd Fret

Minor Second, 1/2 step → (♭2)

Major Second, whole step → (2)   5th Fret

Minor Third, 1 1/2 steps → (♭3)

Major Third, 2 steps → (3)   7th Fret

Perfect Fourth, 2 1/2 steps → (4)

Aug. 4th, Dim. 5th, Tritone; 3 steps → (♭5)   9th Fret

Perfect Fifth, 3 1/2 steps → (5)

Aug. 5th, Minor 6th; 4 steps → (♭6)

Major sixth, 4 1/2 steps → (6)   12th Fret

Minor seventh, 5 steps → (♭7)

Major seventh, 5 1/2 steps → (7)

Octave, 6 steps → (8)   15th Fret

Alphabetical Spelling – Intervals

Alphabetical spelling for intervals is similar to the method used to find correct spelling for major and minor scales. To find the correct spelling for an interval, use the letter sequences shown in Chapter 1, and **count alphabetically**. Counting alphabetically simply means to correspond a number with a letter of the alphabet.

The example below illustrates correct interval spelling. On your bass, play a **perfect 4th** interval (R=1, 4=per 4th) starting from the root A♭. There are two choices of note names: C♯ and D♭. The correct spelling is D♭ because it is four letters away from the root A♭.

1	2	3	4
A♭	B♭	C	D♭

Had we called the note C♯ there would have been two different kinds of C's.

Now find a major sixth interval away from the root B. Is the interval G♯ or A♭? **Count alphabetically** to obtain the answer:

1	2	3	4	5	6	7	8
B	C♯	D♯	E	F♯	G♯	A♯	B

The answer is G♯, because it is six letters away from the root B. Had we called the note A♭, we would have omitted any kind of G, and had two A's. Once you thoroughly memorize the notes on the fretboard and grasp **counting alphabetically**, you will find that this a very simple process.

Overview – Intervals

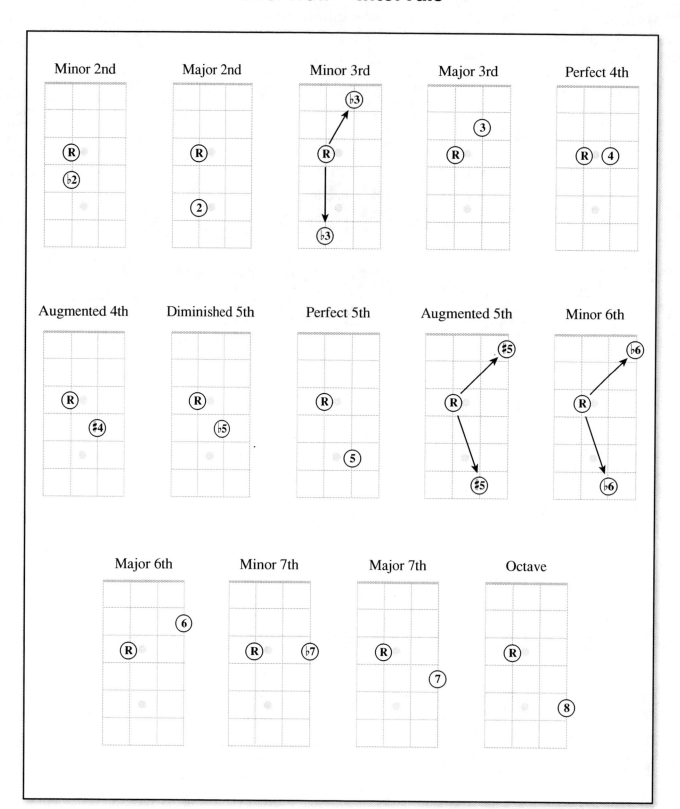

Review Questions

I. Use a pencil to label the notes on each diagram, and label the interval on the space below it. For extra practice, play each interval on your bass and label the notes on the grid.

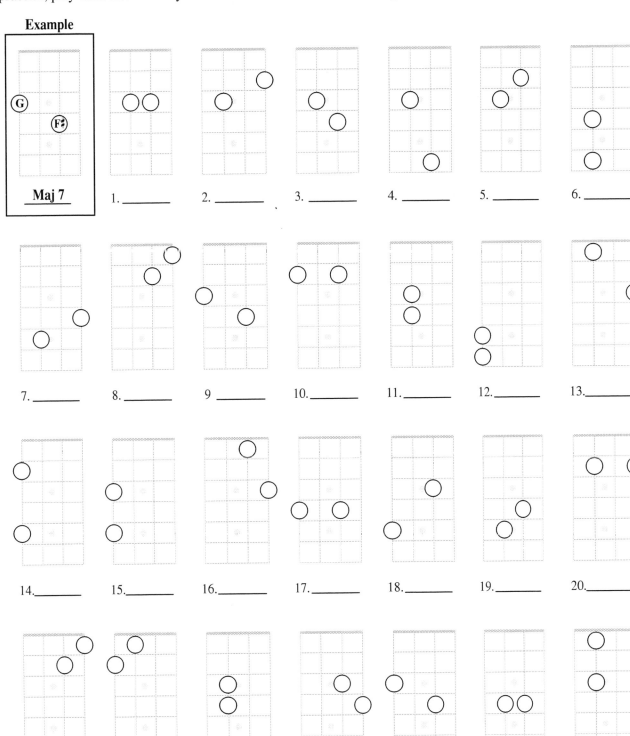

Example

G F#

Maj 7

1. _____   2. _____   3. _____   4. _____   5. _____   6. _____

7. _____   8. _____   9. _____   10. _____   11. _____   12. _____   13. _____

14. _____   15. _____   16. _____   17. _____   18. _____   19. _____   20. _____

21. _____   22. _____   23. _____   24. _____   25. _____   26. _____   27. _____

II. Play each requested interval on your bass, then pencil it in on the blank graph below. Label the note names for extra practice.

Example

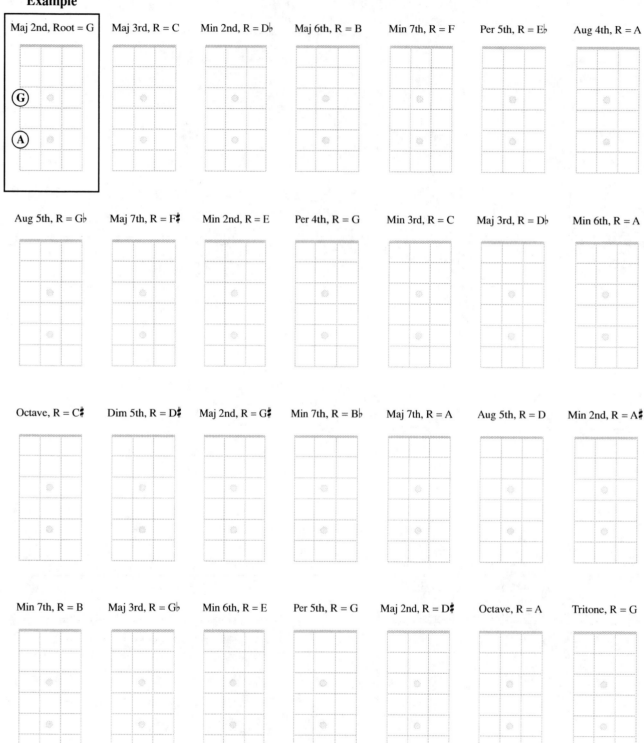

| Maj 2nd, Root = G | Maj 3rd, R = C | Min 2nd, R = D♭ | Maj 6th, R = B | Min 7th, R = F | Per 5th, R = E♭ | Aug 4th, R = A |

| Aug 5th, R = G♭ | Maj 7th, R = F♯ | Min 2nd, R = E | Per 4th, R = G | Min 3rd, R = C | Maj 3rd, R = D♭ | Min 6th, R = A |

| Octave, R = C♯ | Dim 5th, R = D♯ | Maj 2nd, R = G♯ | Min 7th, R = B♭ | Maj 7th, R = A | Aug 5th, R = D | Min 2nd, R = A♯ |

| Min 7th, R = B | Maj 3rd, R = G♭ | Min 6th, R = E | Per 5th, R = G | Maj 2nd, R = D♯ | Octave, R = A | Tritone, R = G |

III. Fill in the blanks.

1. If **A♭** is the root, then _____ is the major second.

2. If **B** is the root, then _____ is the major sixth.

3. If the minor third is **E♭**, then _____ is the root.

4. If the tritone is **E**, then the root is _____.

5. If **F** is the root, then the perfect fourth is _____.

6. If the root is **A**, and the interval is **C♯**, it is called a _____.

7. A minor sixth away from the root **D** is _____.

8. A major third away from **G** is _____.

9. If the root is **F♯**, then the major second is _____.

10. If **B♭** is the root, then the perfect fifth is _____.

11. When **D♭** is the root, and **F** is the interval, this distance is called a _____.

12. If **G** is the minor seventh, then the root is _____.

13. If **A** is the root, then the tritone is _____.

14. If the minor second is **F**, then the root is _____.

15. If the root is _____, then the major third is **G♯**.

16. If the augmented 5th is **C𝄪**, then the root is _____.

17. A major third is equal to _____ steps.

18. A tritone is equal to _____ steps.

19. If the root is **C**, then the minor seventh is _____.

20. An octave is equal to _____ steps.

IV. Name each interval shown on the staff (write each name above the staff). Play each interval on your bass and identify the shape (use note chart and staff chart in the introduction if needed).

V. Write the note on the staff to complete the interval (the root is given). Find the root note on your bass, then play the interval to obtain the answer. Remember to use correct alphabet spelling by counting alphabetically.

49

Chapter Four
Triads – Chord Structure

While it may seem that there are thousands of different chords, each one can break down into one of five different groups. The five different groups are: **Major, Minor, Augmented, Diminished,** and **Suspended.** These qualities are represented by three note chords called **triads.** All examples in this chapter are shown on the root **C,** but may be moved to any of the twelve different notes. After the patterns for the five groups are learned, you will have knowledge of 60 chords. Memorize the correct fingering, chord symbols, and interval structure of each one.

Chords are most often thought of as a cluster of notes played simultaneously, but they still may be considered a chord when they are played in succession. For example, a walking bass line has notes that are played one at a time, but they can outline the notes of a chord that a guitarist or pianist may be playing.

This chapter focuses on **triads** and their **chord symbols, fingerings, interval structure,** and **note names.** Below is an overview of all five groupings. Study it carefully, then proceed to a more detailed view of the chords on the following pages.

	Major	Minor	Augmented	Diminished	Suspended
	C	Cm	C+	Cdim	Csus

Remember that all examples are shown on the root C and should be moved to different roots when the pattern is memorized. By moving a given pattern to another root, it effectively becomes that chord. For example, when the C minor finger pattern is moved to the root Ab, it becomes Ab minor.

Major (R-3-5)

C

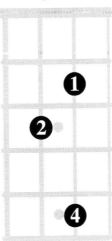

R   3   5

Interval Structure

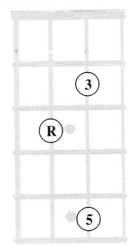

Fingering

The chord symbol for the major triad is represented by a capitalized note name. Chord symbols appear over the measure lines in sheet music and tablature, and are applicable to the guitar, piano, and other rhythm instruments. This triad serves as the tonic chord in a major key, and is composed of the major third and perfect fifth intervals built on the same root.

Alternate Fingering

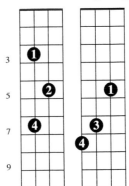

Chord Symbol

C

51

Minor (R-♭3-5)

Cm

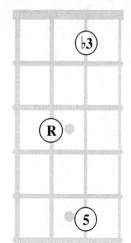

Interval Structure

Fingering

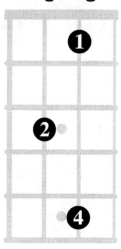

The minor triad is represented by one of three chord symbols shown in the table below. All are interchangeable and refer to the same chord. This triad is also the tonic chord for a minor key, and is composed of the minor third and perfect fifth intervals built on the same root.

Alternate Fingering

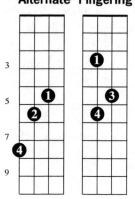

Chord Symbols

Cm
Cmin
C–

Augmented (R-3-♯5)

C+

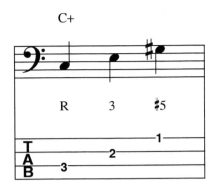

Interval Structure

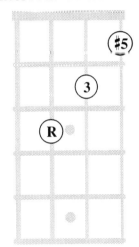

Fingering

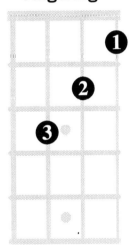

The augmented triad is represented by the root name and the abbreviation "aug," or the plus sign (+). This chord is the same as a major triad with a raised fifth, and is composed of a major third and augmented fifth intervals built on the same root.

Alternate Fingering

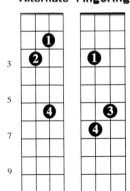

Chord Symbols

Caug
C+

Diminished (R-♭3-♭5)

Cdim

R   ♭3   ♭5

Interval Structure

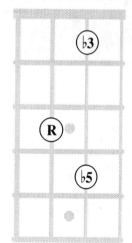

Fingering

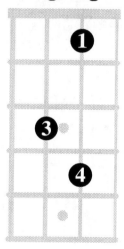

The diminished triad is represented by the abbreviation "dim" or the (○) symbol. This triad is also the same as a minor triad with a flat fifth, and is composed of a minor third and diminished fifth intervals.

Alternate Fingering

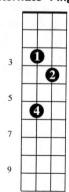

Chord Symbols

Cdim
C○

Suspended (R-4-5)

Csus

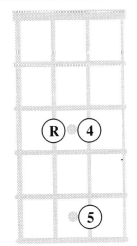

Interval Structure

Fingering

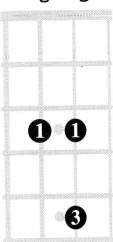

A suspended triad is represented with the root name, and the abbreviation "sus." It is the only triad that contains a fourth interval; the rest contain thirds and fifths.

Alternate Fingering

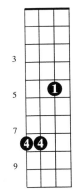

Chord Symbols

Csus

Major and Minor Triad Exercise
Through the Cycle of Fifths

1. Major triads

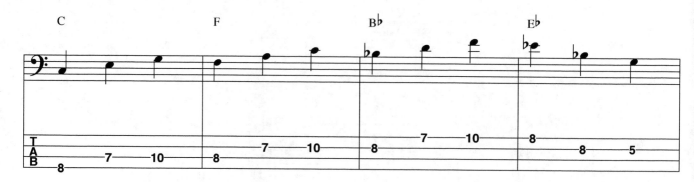

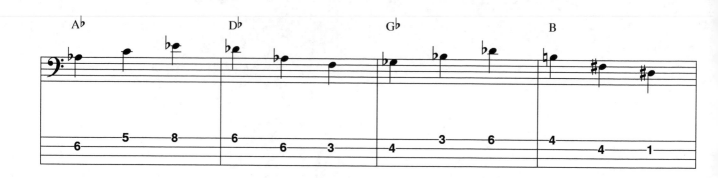

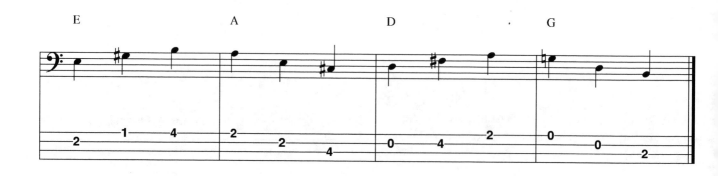

2. Minor triads

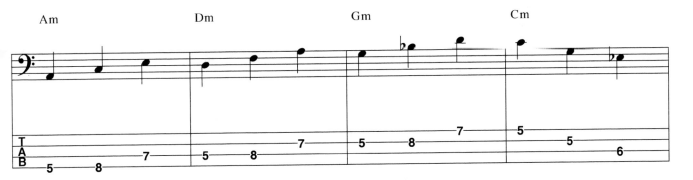

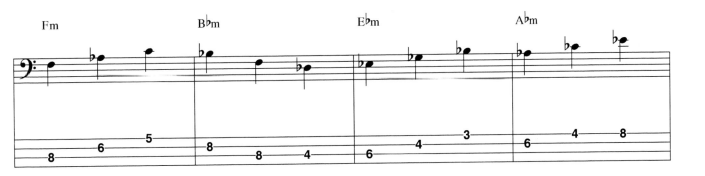

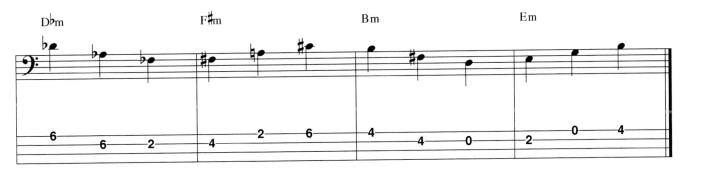

Alphabetical Spellings: Chords

Like intervals and scales, chords must also be spelled correctly. The interval structure of triads and chords are based in thirds, meaning every other note of a scale is played.

A major triad is constructed with a root, third, and fifth, which implies that the second and fourth are skipped. When an interval is skipped, so should a letter of the musical alphabet.

Example 1: C major triad

C	D	E	F	G	A	B	C
R	2	3	4	5	6	7	8

The interval structure of a D minor triad is R-♭3-5, so the correct spelling for this chord would be D, F, and A, not D, F♭ and A. The flatted third (♭3) refers to the lowered F♯-F♮.

Example 2: B diminished chord

B Major Scale:	B	C♯	D♯	E	F♯	G♯	A♯	B
	R	2	3	4	5	6	7	8

The interval structure of a B diminished chord is R-♭3-♭5, so the correct spelling for this chord would be B, D, and F. The flatted third and fifth refer to the lowered major third and the perfect fifth extracted from the major scale, explaining why the correct notes are D and F, and not D♭ and F♭.

Overview – the Five Triad Groups Shown with One Fingering

1. Major

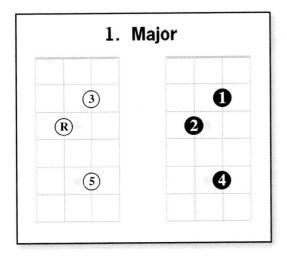

2. Minor

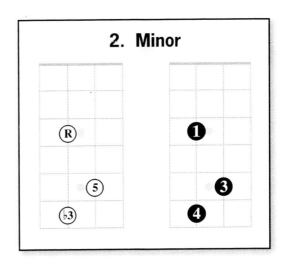

3. Augmented

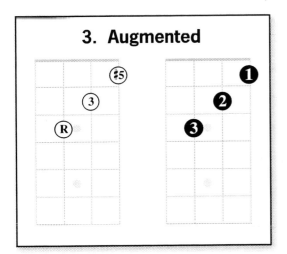

4. Diminished

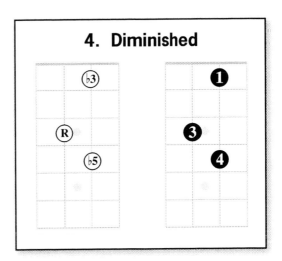

5. Suspended

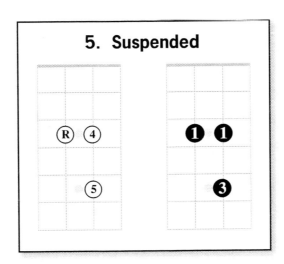

Review Questions

I. Using chord symbols, name each triad shown in each graph below. Play each note on your bass and make sure it matches the examples listed in the chapter.

o = Open string

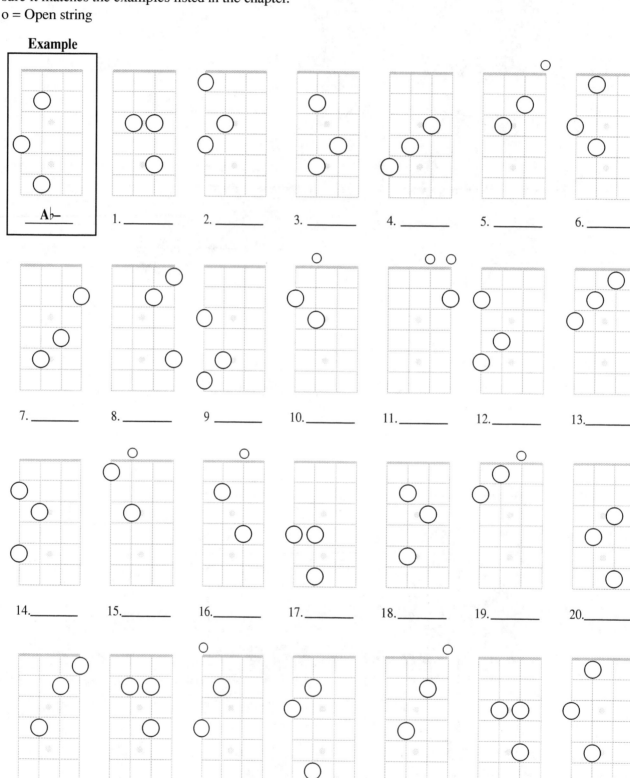

Example

Ab–

1. _____   2. _____   3. _____   4. _____   5. _____   6. _____

7. _____   8. _____   9. _____   10. _____   11. _____   12. _____   13. _____

14. _____   15. _____   16. _____   17. _____   18. _____   19. _____   20. _____

21. _____   22. _____   23. _____   24. _____   25. _____   26. _____   27. _____

II. Play each triad on your bass, then draw it (one octave range, as shown in this chapter) in the fretboard grid below. Remember that each triad has two or more possible fingerings, and use open strings wherever necessary. There are several correct answers for each one, but only one answer will be provided in the answer key.

Example

Major, Root = A	Minor, R = F	Aug, R = B♭	Major, R = B	Dim, R = G	Sus, R = E♭	Major, R = D
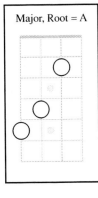						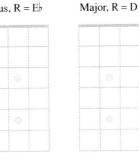

Minor, R = G♭	Dim, R = A♯	Aug, R = E	Sus, R = G	Major, R = F	Major, R = D♭	Minor, R = E♭
					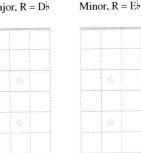	

Dim, R = D♭	Sus, R = G♯	Major, R = B	Aug, R = B♭	Major, R = A♭	Minor, R = A	Aug, R = F♯

Minor, R = B	Aug, R = E♭	Dim, R = C	Major, R = G	Sus, R = D♯	Minor, R = D	Major, R = G♯
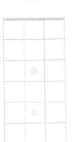						

III. Using chord symbols, name each triad shown below.

IV. Write the notes on the staff to complete the triad (the root is given). Use correct alphabet spelling. Play each triad on your bass at the end of each exercise.

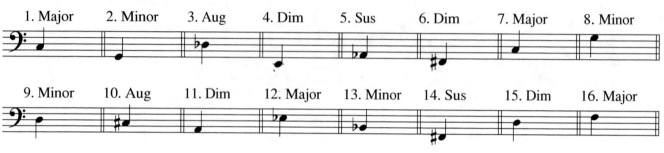

V. True/False, short answer.

1. **C, E,** and **G** make up a(n) _____ chord.

2. An F aug chord contains the notes _____, _____, and _____.

3. Name the two intervals that comprise a suspended chord.

4. **A, C,** and **E** complete a(n) _____ chord.

5. T or F. The term "triad" may be substituted with the word "chord".

6. T or F. All triads contain a root, third, and fifth, except for diminished.

7. A Gmin chord contains the notes _____, _____, and _____.

8. Name the two intervals that make up a major triad.

9. **F♯, A♯,** and **C𝄪** complete the _____ chord.

10. The five different groups of triads are _____, _____, _____, _____, and _____.

11. T or F. A♭, C♯, and E♭ make up an A♭ major triad.

12. T or F. The chord symbol for diminished is a little hollow circle.

13. T or F. The chord symbol for augmented is the plus sign (+).

14. T or F. A major triad has no chord symbol; only the root note is shown.

15. T or F. All triads must start from the root to actually be considered a chord.

16. A Bsus triad contains the notes _____, _____, and _____.

17. An A♭min triad contains the notes _____, _____, and _____.

18. Name the two intervals that comprise a minor triad.

19. The chord symbol for a minor triad is _____.

20. T or F. The correct spelling for a Gmin triad is **G-B♭-D.**

21. T or F. The correct spelling for a Caug triad is **C-E-A♭.**

22. T or F. The correct spelling for a D♭dim triad is **D♭-E-G.**

23. T or F. The correct spelling for a Bmaj triad is **B-D♯-F♯.**

24. T or F. The correct spelling for an A♭(sus) triad is **A♭-C♯-E♭.**

25. T or F. The correct spelling for an Emaj triad is **E-G♯-B.**

Chapter Five
Seventh Chords

Seventh chords are the next extension of triads. All of the seventh chords shown in this chapter contain one of the triads shown in Chapter Four with a major or minor seventh interval added to each. Once you have read through this chapter and played all of the examples on the root C of your bass, practice the seventh chords on different roots of the neck. These chords are also the premise for 9th, 11th, and 13th chords.

Major Seventh (R-3-5-7)

Cmaj7

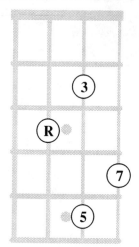

Interval Structure

Fingering

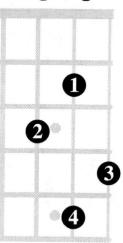

The interval structure of this chord is a major third, perfect fifth, and major seventh all played on the same root. It serves as the tonic chord for major keys.

Alternate Fingering

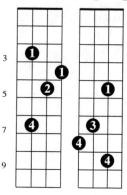

Chord Symbols

C△7
C△
Cmaj
Cmaj7

Dominant Seventh (R-3-5-♭7)

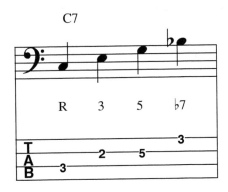

Interval Structure

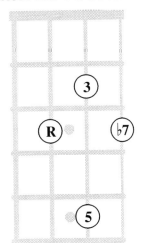

Fingering

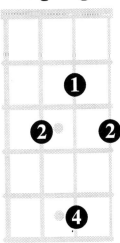

The interval structure is composed of a major third, perfect fifth, and minor seventh based on the root 'C'. Note that the chord symbol is the C triad symbol, plus the number seven. The number seven indicates the minor seventh interval.

Alternate Fingering

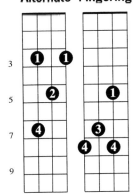

Chord Symbol

C7

Minor Seventh (R-♭3-5-♭7)

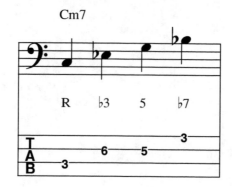

Cm7

Interval Structure

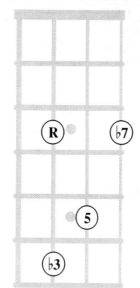

Fingering

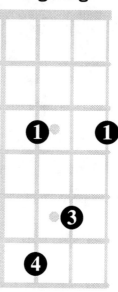

This chord is a combination of the minor third, perfect fifth, and minor seventh intervals played on the same root. A minor seventh is the tonic chord in a minor key.

Alternate Fingering

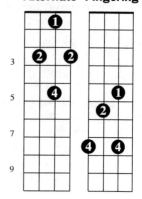

Chord Symbols

C-7
Cmin7
Cm7

Cm(maj7)

| R | ♭3 | 5 | 7 |

Interval Structure

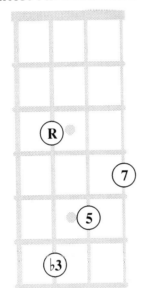

Fingering

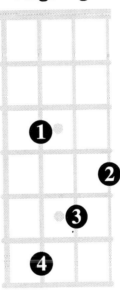

The interval structure of this chord is composed of a minor third, perfect fifth, and a major seventh.

Alternate Fingering

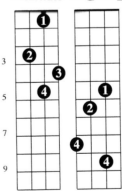

Chord Symbols

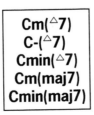

Cm(△7)
C-(△7)
Cmin(△7)
Cm(maj7)
Cmin(maj7)

Augmented Maj 7th (R-3-♯5-7)

C+(maj7)

R   3   ♯5   7

Interval Structure

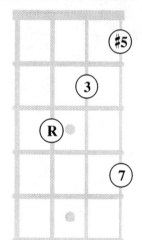

Fingering

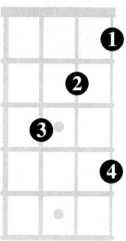

This chord is composed of the major third, augmented fifth, and major seventh intervals built on the same root. Play this chord on the root C, then practice moving the pattern to different roots to form a new chord.

Alternate Fingering

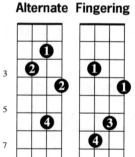

Chord Symbols

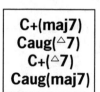

C+(maj7)
Caug(△7)
C+(△7)
Caug(maj7)

Augmented 7th (R-3-♯5-♭7)

C+7

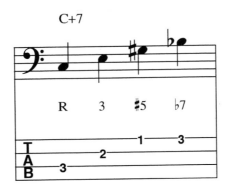

Interval Structure

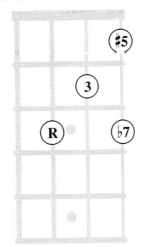

Fingering

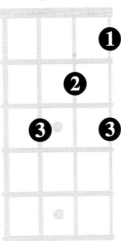

This chord is composed of the major third, augmented fifth, and minor seventh intervals built on the same root.

Alternate Fingering

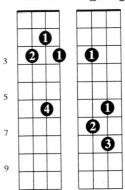

Chord Symbols

Caug7
C+7

Diminished (R-♭3-♭5-♭♭7)

Cdim7

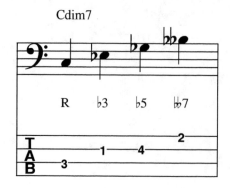

Interval Structure

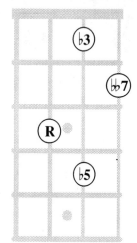

Fingering

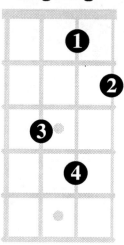

This seventh chord is composed of the minor third, diminished fifth, and fully diminished seventh intervals. A fully diminished seventh is a flat-flat seventh (♭♭7).

Alternate Fingering

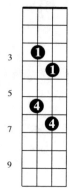

Chord Symbols

Cdim7
C°7

Half-Diminished (R-♭3-♭5-♭7)

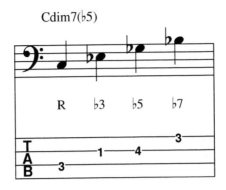

Cdim7(♭5)

Interval Structure

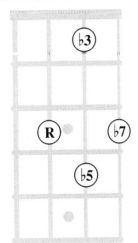

Fingering

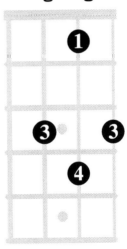

The interval structure of this chord is a minor third, diminished fifth, and a minor seventh.

Alternate Fingering

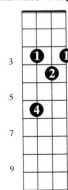

Chord Symbols

Cmin7(♭5)
Cø7
Cø

Suspended 7th (R-4-5-♭7)

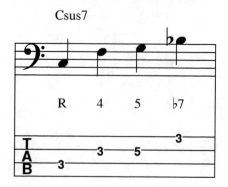

Csus7

R   4   5   ♭7

Interval Structure

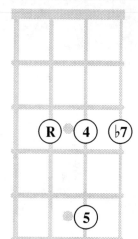

Fingering

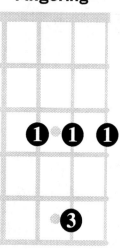

This chord is composed of a perfect fourth, perfect fifth, and a minor seventh.

Alternate Fingering

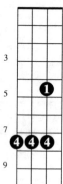

Chord Symbols

Csus7
C7sus

Table of Triads & 7th Chords

Chord Group	Interval Structure	Chord Symbols
Major Triad	R-3-5	C
Minor Triad	R-♭3-5	Cm, C-, Cminor
Augmented Triad	R-3-♯5	C+, Caug
Diminished Triad	R-♭3-♭5	Cdim, C°
Suspended Triad	R-4-5	Csus, Csus4
Major Sixth	R-3-5-6	C6
Minor Sixth	R-♭3-5-6	C-6, Cm6, Cminor6, Cmin6
Major Seventh	R-3-5-7	C△, C△7, Cmaj7, Cmaj
Dominant Seventh	R-3-5-♭7	C7
Minor Seventh	R-♭3 5-♭7	C-7, Cmin7, Cm7
Minor/Major Seventh	R-♭3-5-7	Cm(△7), C-(^7), Cmin(△7), Cm(maj7)
Augmented/Major Seventh	R-3-♯5-7	C+(maj7), C+(△7), Caug(maj7), Caug(maj7)
Augmented Seventh	R-3-♯5-♭7	Caug7, C+7
Diminished	R-♭3-♭5-♭♭7	C°7, Cdim7
Half-Diminished	R-♭3-♭5-♭7	Cø, Cø7, Cm7(♭5)
Suspended Seventh	R-4-5-♭7	Csus7

Overview – Seventh Chords Shown in Chapter 5

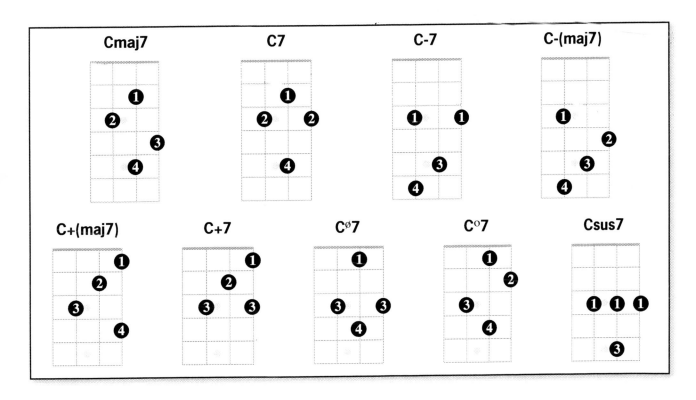

Review Questions

I. Play each chord on your bass, then plot it on the graph below. For extra practice, label the note names on each chord.

Example

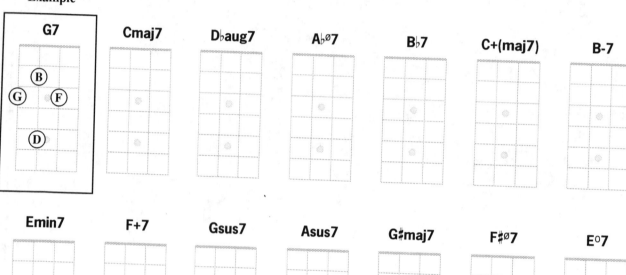

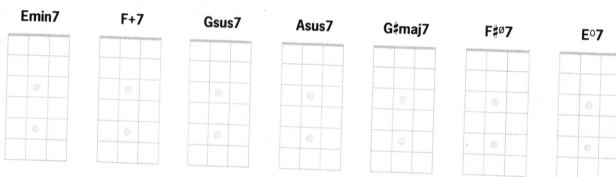

I. Using the correct chord symbols, name each seventh chord represented on the grid. Play each chord on your bass and label the notes. Use correct alphabetical spellings.

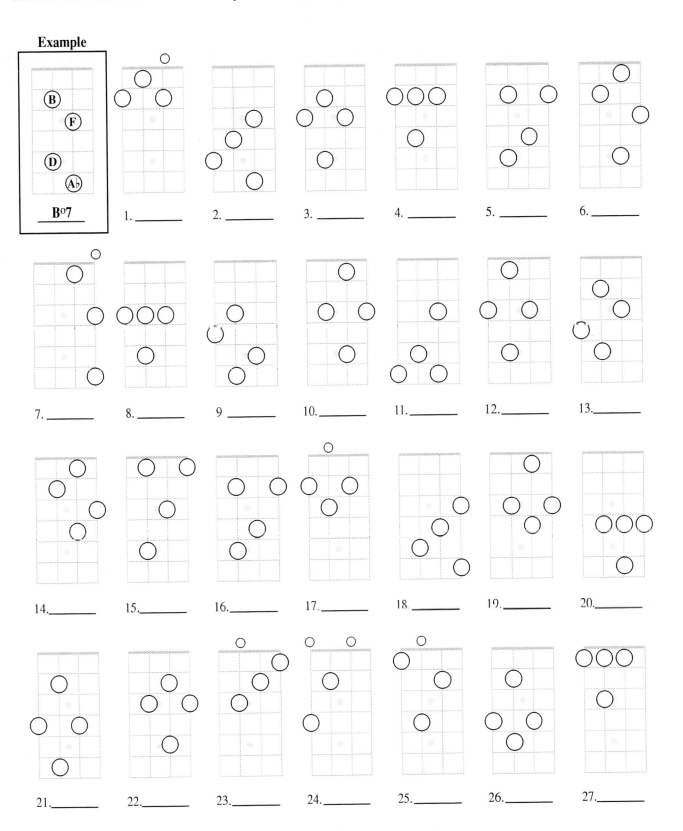

III. Play each example on your bass, then identify the finger pattern to obtain the chord. Write the answer in chord symbol form above the staff. Use the "Notes Of The Staff" chart in the introduction if necessary.

IV. Label the notes on the staff for each seventh chord given.

1. Cmaj 7   2. Ab+7   3. B-7   4. G7   5. Ab-7   6. Fdim7   7. Dmaj7   8. Eb7

9. B-(maj7)   10. F#+7   11. Esus7   12. A7   13. Bb7   14. Gmin7   15. Em7   16. C+(maj7)

V. True or False

1. **C-E-G-Bb** is a C7 chord.

2. The interval structure of an augmented seventh chord is **R-3-#5-b7**.

3. The chord symbol for a C major seventh chord is C7.

4. A Gmin7 chord is made up of the notes **G-Bb-D-F**.

5. The interval structure of a suspended seventh chord is **R-4-5-b7**.

VI. Fill in the blanks.

1. _____ is the perfect fifth in a G7 chord.

2. _____ is the minor seventh in an Ebmin7 chord.

3. If D is the third and Ab is the minor seventh, then the root of this dominant seventh chord is_____ .

4. The chord symbol for an F dominant seventh chord is_____ .

5. If Bb is the minor third and F# is the major seventh, then the root of this minor/major seventh chord is _____ .

6. The chord symbol for C# fully diminished is _____ .

7. _____ is the major seventh in an Abmaj7 chord.

8. _____ is the diminished fifth in a C# fully diminished chord.

9. The chord symbol for B minor seventh is _____ .

10. The three intervals that compose an augmented major seventh chord are _____ , _____ , and_____ .

Chapter Six
Chords of the Major and Minor Scale

The diatonic chords of the major and minor scales are one of the most important harmonic ideas that a bassist should know. These chord formulas determine the chord structures to literally thousands of songs in pop, rock, country, top 40, R&B, gospel, and jazz. Knowing this formula can take the work out of playing your instrument, and give you an instant edge to playing by ear. This chapter will fully utilize interval, scale, triad, and seventh chord relationships, so make sure that you have completed the worksheets for each of the preceding chapters. Listed to the right is the entire formula for the diatonic chords of the major scale. This is a set idea that should be memorized.

Each of the Roman numerals represents a note and its corresponding chord, starting from the lowest note of the scale to the highest. The quality (major, minor, or diminished) listed below the Roman numeral refers to the type of triad to be built upon the different scale degrees (Roman numerals). To apply this concept to the bass, several different steps must be considered. First, play a one octave C major scale on your bass, and recite the names of each note as you play through it (ex. C-D-E, etc.). Each note in this scale will represent the root of the triads listed above in the Roman numeral formula to their corresponding degrees. Since the root of the C major scale is C, and the Roman numeral formula for the I chord is major, then the first chord is C major. The second note of a C major scale is D, and the Roman numeral formula for the second note of the D scale is a minor triad, so the chord is D minor. This pattern continues for each remaining note of the scale, applied to the Roman Numeral chord formula shown above. Memorize the Roman numeral formula above, and you will be able to quickly pick out the chords of the major scale in any of the 12 keys. Remember to start the process by playing the one octave scale, then apply the formula to each note of the scale. Always count the root as I, then count up the scale. There are seven different letter note names in any major or minor scale, and there are seven different chords in the formula.

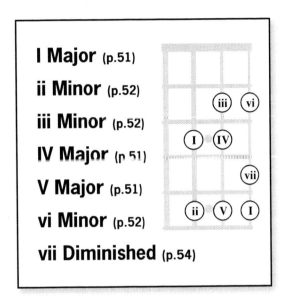

I Major (p.51)

ii Minor (p.52)

iii Minor (p.52)

IV Major (p.51)

V Major (p.51)

vi Minor (p.52)

vii Diminished (p.54)

C   Dm   Em   F   G   Am   Bdim   C

The chords of the major scale are also referred to as the "harmonized major scale" or "diatonic chords of the scale." Each of these terms are correct, and may be used interchangeably. These chords are taken from the notes of the major scale itself. For example, in the chord formula for the C major scale, the I chord C major is composed of the notes **C, E,** and **G**; all of which are contained in the C major scale (CDEFGABC). The ii chord (Dmin) contains the notes **D, F,** and **A**, which are also in the key of C major (CDEFGABC). The same goes for the iii chord Emin (CDEFGABC) and so on. Once again, this concept is referred to as "harmonizing the major scale" because all of the notes are within a particular scale, in this case C major. To further illustrate how this works, let's look at chords of the major scale for the key of **E♭**.

I = E♭maj (E♭, G, and B♭)

ii = Fmin (F, A♭, and C)

iii = Gmin (G,B♭, and D)

IV = A♭maj (A♭, C, and E♭)

V = B♭maj (B♭, D, and F)

vi = Cmin (C, E♭, and G)

vii = Ddim (D, F, and A♭)

Steps to Understanding the Chord Formula (Major Scale)

1. Memorize the Roman numeral formula: I (maj), ii (min), iii (min), IV (maj), V (maj), vi (min), vii (dim)

2. Play through a C major scale, and recite the note name and corresponding Roman numeral chord.

3. Play individual chords built on each degree of the scale.

4. Practice skipping through different chords within the scale (ex. Cmaj, Emin, Amin, etc.). Think of the chords as independent entities within the frame of a major scale.

5. Adapt this process to the remaining 11 major keys.

The E♭ major scale contains the notes E♭, F, G, A♭, B♭, C, and D. Every one of the notes taken from the seven chords shown above will fall into this scale.

Now let's apply the formula to the key of A Major. First, play a one octave A major scale on the fifth fret of the E string. As you ascend and descend through the scale, recite the name of each note.

A B C♯ D E F♯ G♯

Now apply the chord formula to the scale degrees:

I major = Amaj

ii minor = Bmin

iii minor = C♯min

IV major = Dmaj

V major = Emaj

vi minor = F♯min

vii diminished = G♯dim

Now that the chords of the A major scale are evident, progressions in the key of A major can be played.

Example 1: I-IV-V progression in the key of A major.
I major = A major
IV major = D major
V major – E major

A, D, and E are the correct chords for this progression.

Example 2: I-vi-ii-V progression in the key of A major.
I major = A
vi minor = F♯ min
ii minor = B min
V major-- E maj

A, F♯min, Bmin, and E are the correct chords for this progression.

The table below shows the chord formula applied to the twelve major keys.

I Major	ii minor	iii minor	IV Major	V Major	vi minor	vii dimin.
C	Dmin	Emin	F	G	Amin	Bdim
F	Gmin	Amin	B♭	C	Dmin	Edim
B♭	Cmin	Dmin	E♭	F	Gmin	Adim
E♭	Fmin	Gmin	A♭	B♭	Cmin	Ddim
A♭	B♭min	Cmin	D♭	E♭	Fmin	Gdim
D♭	E♭min	Fmin	G♭	A♭	B♭min	Cdim
F♯	G♯min	A♯min	B	C♯	D♯min	E♯dim
B	C♯min	D♯min	E	F♯	G♯min	A♯dim
E	F♯min	G♯min	A	B	C♯min	D♯dim
A	Bmin	C♯min	D	E	F♯min	G♯dim
D	Emin	F♯min	G	A	Bmin	C♯dim
G	Amin	Bmin	C	D	Emin	F♯dim

This system can also be expanded to seventh chords.

Imaj7	ii – 7	iii – 7	IVmaj7	V7	vi – 7	vii⌀7
Major 7th	Minor 7th	Minor 7th	Major 7th	Dom 7th	Minor 7th	Half Dim 7th

Imaj7	**ii – 7**	**iii – 7**	**IVmaj7**	**V7**	**vi – 7**	**vii⌀7**
Cmaj7	Dmin7	Emin7	Fmaj7	G7	Amin7	B⌀7
Fmaj7	Gmin7	Amin7	B♭maj7	C7	Dmin7	E⌀7
B♭maj7	Cmin7	Dmin7	E♭maj7	F7	Gmin7	A⌀7
E♭maj7	Fmin7	Gmin7	A♭maj7	B♭7	Cmin7	D⌀7
A♭maj7	B♭min7	Cmin7	D♭maj7	E♭7	Fmin7	G⌀7
D♭maj7	E♭min7	Fmin7	G♭maj7	A♭7	B♭min7	C⌀7
F♯maj7	G♯min7	A♯min7	Bmaj7	C♯7	D♯min7	E♯⌀7
Bmaj7	C♯min7	D♯min7	Emaj7	F♯7	G♯min7	A♯⌀7
Emaj7	F♯min7	G♯min7	Amaj7	B7	C♯min7	D♯⌀7
Amaj7	Bmin7	C♯min7	Dmaj7	E7	F♯min 7	G♯⌀7
Dmaj7	Emin7	F♯min7	Gmaj7	A7	Bmin7	C♯⌀7
Gmaj7	Amin7	Bmin7	Cmaj7	D7	Emin7	F♯⌀7

Exercise – 7th Chords of the G Major Scale

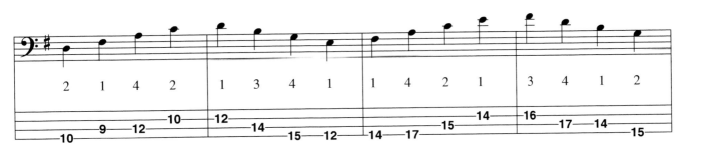

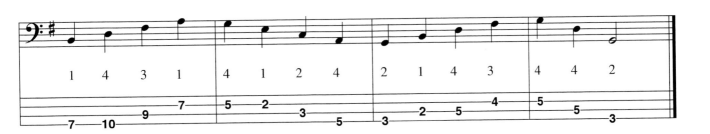

Chord Formula for the Minor Scale

Chapter Three discussed how minor scales are relative to major. This concept can be applied to the major scale formula to find the minor scale formula. Since the relative minor scale is built on the sixth note in the major key, the sixth note of a major scale will now become the i in the relative minor key. The example chart for the chords of the minor scale will skip the triad formula and begin with the seventh chord formula. If you would like to find the triads of the minor scale, extract the basic triad from each seventh chord in the formula. The result will be i-iidim-III-iv-v-VI-VII.

Major Scale Formula Compared with the Minor Scale

Major Scale Formula												
Cmaj7	D-7	E-7	Fmaj7	G7	A-7	B∅7	Cmaj7	D-7	E-7	Fmaj7	G7	Am7
Imaj7	ii-7	iii-7	IVmaj7	V7	vi-7	vii∅7	Imaj7	ii-7	iii-7	IVmaj7	V7	vi-7

Minor Scale Chord Formula												
					i-7	ii∅7	IIImaj7	iv-7	v-7	VImaj7	VII7	i-7
					A-7	B∅7	Cmaj7	D-7	E-7	Fmaj7	G7	A-7

Notice that the quality of each chord did not change (minor 7, maj7, etc.), only the Roman numeral did. This progression imposed on top of the one octave minor scale illustrates how the pattern is relative to the major scale.

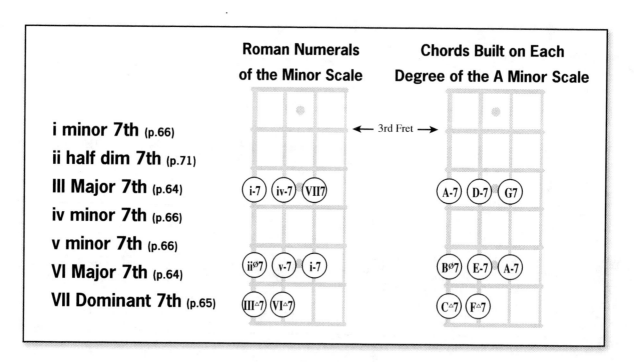

i minor 7th (p.66)

ii half dim 7th (p.71)

III Major 7th (p.64)

iv minor 7th (p.66)

v minor 7th (p.66)

VI Major 7th (p.64)

VII Dominant 7th (p.65)

Using the right column for the chords of the scale, we now have a group of chords to draw from for the key of A minor.

Steps to Understanding the Chord Formula
(Minor Scale)

1. Memorize the Roman numeral formula.
   i (min), ii (dim), III (maj), iv (min), v (min), VI (maj), VII (maj).

2. Play through an A minor scale, and recite each note name and corresponding Roman numeral chord.

3. Build the triad or seventh chord on each degree of the scale (scale note is the root of the chord).

4. Practice skipping through different chords within the scale (ex. A-, D-, Bdim, Em, etc.). Think of the chords as independent entities within the frame of a minor scale.

5. Adapt this process to the remaining 11 minor keys.

Ear Training

Being able to hear and play chord progressions should be the goal of every bassist. Now that you have gained understanding of intervals, scales, and chords, you must use them to think analytically and musically.

Ear Training Review

1. **Be able to recognize intervals by ear.** For practice, record a 60 minute tape of various intervals on the root C. Record, while playing each interval three times, then say the name at the end of the cycle. Repeat. Play the tape back and try to guess the interval before its name is spoken.

2. **Be able to recognize the major and minor scale by ear.**

3. **Be able to recognize triads and seventh chords by ear.** Make taped examples of each and try to guess them. Break down each one individually and listen for the sounds of the interval structure.

4. **Be able to recognize the chords of the major and minor scale by ear.**

Hearing and Analyzing by Ear

1. Listen for the tonal center (root) of the key.

2. Determine whether the music is in a major or minor key. Reference the appropriate scale once this is determined.

3. Listen to the root movement of chords. This is similar to listening for tonality in that you are concentrating on the strongest note of a chord or triad instead of the root of a major or minor scale. As chords move through a song, assimilate root movement between two chords to the sounds of a two note interval shown in Chapter One.

4. After the root movement is determined, determine whether it fits the structure of a major or minor scale. Then apply the chords to their corresponding degrees and see which ones match up. Listen to the overall chord quality of each one (maj, min, aug, dim, or sus), and compare with the chords of the major or minor scale.

Review Questions

I. Short answer and True/False.

1. The ii chord in the key of A♭ major is _____.

2. The vii chord in the key of F♯ major is _____.

3. If B minor is the iii chord, then the root of the major key is _____.

4. T or F. The augmented triad is built on the sixth degree of the major scale formula.

5. T or F. The diminished triad is built on the seventh degree of the major scale formula.

6. If Gmin7 is the vi chord, then the tonic chord is _____.

7. If Cmaj7 is the IV chord, then the tonic chord is _____.

8. If B♭maj7, Gmin7, and Fmaj7 are in the key of F major, then transpose the progression to the key of G major. _____, _____, and _____.

9. Name the chords in a vi-ii-V-I progression in the key of E♭ major. _____, _____, _____, and _____.

10. The ii and V chords in the key of D♭ major are _____ and _____.

11. T or F. The seventh chord built on the seventh degree of the major scale formula is a fully diminished seventh chord.

12. T or F. There are three different minor chords in the major scale chord formula (triads).

13. T or F. There are three different major chords in the minor scale chord formula (triads).

14. T or F. There are three different minor chords in the minor scale chord formula (triads).

15. T or F. There are three different major chords in the major scale chord formula (triads).

16. T or F. The triad chord formula for major contains two minor triads.

17. The quality of the VI chord in the minor scale formula is _____.

18. The quality of the ii chord in the minor scale formula is _____.

19. If Amin, Cmaj7, Dmin7, and Bdim (vi, Imaj7, ii-7, and viidim) are in the key of C major, transpose them to the key of F major. _____, _____, _____, and _____.

20. The major seventh chords in the key of E major are Emaj7 and _____.

21. The minor seventh chords in the key of F♯ major are G♯min7, _____, and _____.

22. The major seventh chords in the key of A minor are Cmaj7 and _____.

23. The dominant seventh chord falls on the _____ degree of the major scale formula.

24. The dominant seventh chord falls on the _____ degree of the minor scale formula.

25. The diminished triad falls on the _____ degree of the major scale formula.

26. The diminished triad falls on the _____ degree of the minor scale formula.

27. T or F. All songs follow the chord formulas listed in this book.

28. T or F. Songwriters and composers only write songs using the chords of the major and minor scale.

29. T or F. The ii -V7 progression in the key of A major is Bmin and E7.

30. T or F. The V17-v7-i pattern in the key of G minor is A-7, D7, and Gmin.

31. T or F. The three different chord qualities that are found in the chords of major scale (triad formula) are Major, Minor, and Diminished.

32. T or F. The three different chord qualities that are found in the chords of the minor scale (triad formula) are Major, Minor, and Diminished.

33. The only major key that G7 and and Bdim can be found in is _____.

34. The only minor key that Gdim and Cmin can be found in is _____.

35. T or F. The V chord in the key of G minor is Dm.

36. The iiim7-IVmaj7-V7-vim7-iim7-Imaj7 progression in the key of B♭ major is _____, _____, _____, _____, _____, and _____.

37. T or F. Gmin7, Adim, and B♭maj7 are found in the keys of B♭ major and G minor.

38. T or F. Emaj7, D♯dim, and Amaj7 are found in the keys of E major and A major.

39. T or F. B7, C♯min7, and Amaj7 are found in the keys of E major and C♯ minor.

40. The i -VI-VII chords in the key of B minor are _____, _____, and _____.

II. Name the 7th chords of each scale below. Write the chords in each blank circle shown.

Final Review

I. Name each of the intervals, triads, and seventh chords listed below.

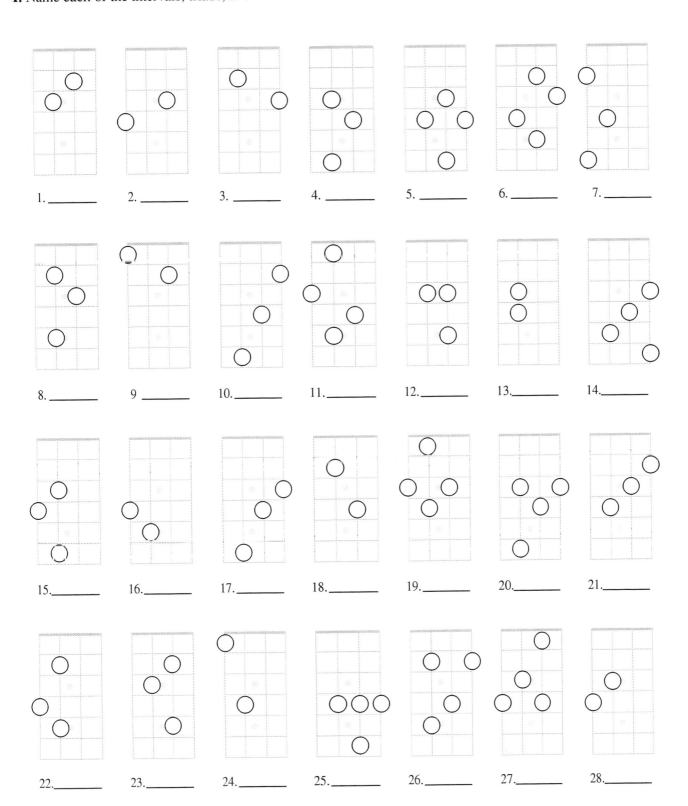

1. _____
2. _____
3. _____
4. _____
5. _____
6. _____
7. _____

8. _____
9. _____
10. _____
11. _____
12. _____
13. _____
14. _____

15. _____
16. _____
17. _____
18. _____
19. _____
20. _____
21. _____

22. _____
23. _____
24. _____
25. _____
26. _____
27. _____
28. _____

II. Fill each requested interval, triad, or seventh chord on the grids below. Use any fingering necessary to fit the notes within the six fret span of the grid.

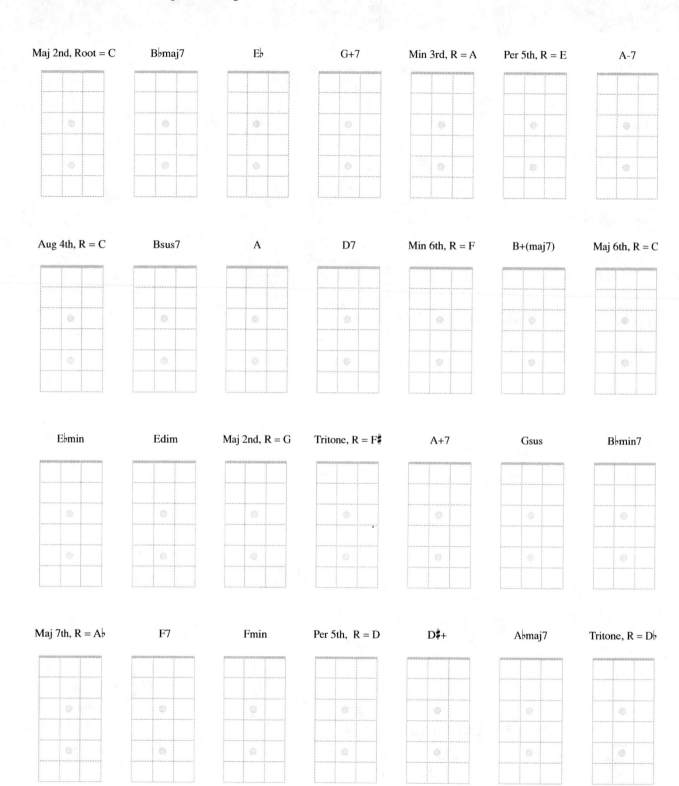

| Maj 2nd, Root = C | B♭maj7 | E♭ | G+7 | Min 3rd, R = A | Per 5th, R = E | A-7 |

| Aug 4th, R = C | Bsus7 | A | D7 | Min 6th, R = F | B+(maj7) | Maj 6th, R = C |

| E♭min | Edim | Maj 2nd, R = G | Tritone, R = F♯ | A+7 | Gsus | B♭min7 |

| Maj 7th, R = A♭ | F7 | Fmin | Per 5th, R = D | D♯+ | A♭maj7 | Tritone, R = D♭ |

III. Name the notes of each major and minor scale listed below. Use correct spelling and be sure the each of the seven letters of the musical alphabet are represented.

1. G Major: ____ ____ ____ ____ ____ ____

2. A♭ Major: ____ ____ ____ ____ ____ ____ ____

3. B Major: ____ ____ ____ ____ ____ ____ ____

4. B♭ Major: ____ ____ ____ ____ ____ ____ ____

5. A Minor: ____ ____ ____ ____ ____ ____ ____

6. D Minor: ____ ____ ____ ____ ____ ____ ____

7. G♯ Minor: ____ ____ ____ ____ ____ ____ ____

8. F Minor: ____ ____ ____ ____ ____ ____ ____

IV. List all of the notes from each major and minor scale on the fret grids below. Circle the roots.

F major　　**E♭ major**　　**G minor**　　**B♭ minor**

V. Short answer, fill in the blanks.

1. If **C** is the root, then _____ is the major second.
2. If the minor sixth is **F**, then _____ is the root.
3. If the tritone is **D♯**, then the root is _____.
4. If **A♭** is the root, then the perfect fifth is _____.
5. If the root is **G**, and the interval is **D**, this distance is called a _____.
6. A minor third away from the root **C♯** is _____.
7. If **F♯** is the major seventh, then the root is _____.
8. If the minor seventh is **E♭**, then the root is _____.
9. If the root is _____, then the major third is **E**.
10. If the augmented 5th is **D𝄪**, then the root is _____.
11. A major sixth is equal to _____ steps.
12. A perfect fourth is equal to _____ steps.
13. Find the root of the major scale that contains the notes **G, F♯, C♯, A, E, B,** and **D**.
14. Find the root of the major scale that contains the notes **B♭, D, F, G, A♭, C,** and **E♭**.
15. The sixth note of a **B** major scale is _____.
16. The fifth note of a **C** major scale is _____.
17. **A♭** is the fifth note of the _____ major scale.
18. **G** is the second note of a(n) _____ major scale.
19. The _____ major scale has three sharps.
20. Name the three notes that are sharped in an **A** major scale: _____, _____, _____.
21. The _____ major scale has two sharps.
22. Name the intervals of a major scale that are major in quality _____, _____, _____, and _____.
23. Name the intervals of a major scale that are perfect in quality _____, _____.
24. The relative minor scale of **G** major is _____.
25. The relative minor scale of **E♭** major is _____.
26. If **D** is the root of the minor scale, then the relative major is _____.
27. If **A♭** is the root of the minor scale, then _____ is the relative major scale.
28. **B♭** minor and _____ share the same key signature of five flats.
29. The _____ major scale has five flats.
30. **A** is the fourth note of the _____ minor scale.
31. Name the interval of a minor scale that is major in quality.
32. Name the intervals of a minor scale that are "perfect" in quality _____, _____.
33. **C♯, E,** and **G** make up a(n) _____ chord.
34. An Aaug chord contains the notes _____, _____, and _____.
35. Name the two intervals that comprise a diminished chord.
36. **A, C♯,** and **E♯** complete a(n) _____ chord.
37. An Fmin chord contains the notes _____, _____, and _____.
38. Name the two intervals that make up a major triad.
39. **F♯, A,** and **C** complete the _____ chord.
40. The five different groups of triads are _____, _____, _____, _____, and _____.
41. A Dsus triad contains the notes _____, _____, and _____.
42. An E major triad contains the notes _____, _____, and _____.
43. Name the two intervals that comprise a minor triad.

90

44. The chord symbol for an augmented triad is _____.

45. _____ is the perfect fifth in a G7 chord.

46. _____ is the minor seventh in an D♭min7 chord.

47. If **A** is the third and **E♭** is the minor seventh, then the root of this dominant seventh chord is _____.

48. The chord symbol for a F♯ dominant seventh chord is _____.

49. If **C** is the minor third and **G♯** is the major seventh, then the root of this minor/major seventh chord is _____.

50. The chord symbol for E fully diminished is _____.

51. The only major key that A7 and and C♯dim can be found in is _____.

52. The only minor key that Edim and Dmin can be found in is _____.

53. The iiim7-IVmaj7-V7-vim7-iim7-Imaj7 progression in the key of A♭ major is _____, _____, _____, _____, _____, and _____.

54. The i-v-VII chords in the key of C minor are_____, _____, and _____.

55. The only major key that E♭7 and and D♭maj7 can be found in is _____.

56. The only minor key that E♯dim and A♯min can be found in is _____.

57. The iim7-IVmaj7-V7-vim7-Imaj7 progression in the key of E♭ major is _____, _____, _____, _____, and _____.

58. The i-iv-v chords in the key of B minor are _____, _____, and _____.

59. The iiim7-IVmaj7-V7-vim7-iim7-Imaj7 progression in the key of G major is _____, _____, _____, _____, and _____.

60. The i-VI-v chords in the key of A minor are_____, _____, and _____.

VI. True or False

1. A C minor scale contains three sharps in the key signature.

2. The relative minor scale of B♭ major is B♭ minor.

3. The four accidentals in an A♭ major scale are **A♭, A♯, D♭,** and **E♭.**

4. There are two flats in the key of G♯ minor.

5. Every key signature represents one major and one minor key.

6. There are three flats in the key of C minor.

7. The correct spelling for an Amin triad is **A-C-E♭.**

8. The correct spelling for a Baug triad is **B-D♯-F♯.**

9. The correct spelling for an Gsus triad is **G-C-D.**

10. The correct spelling for a Ddim triad is **D-F-A.**

11. **B♭-D-F♯-A♭** is a **B♭7** chord.

12. The interval structure of an augmented major seventh chord is R-3-♯5-7.

13. The chord symbol for a D major seventh chord is D7.

14. An Fmin7 chord is made up of the notes **F-A♭-C-E.**

15. The interval structure of a major seventh chord is R-3-5-7.

16. An A major scale contains two sharps in the key signature.

17. There are five flats in a B♭ major scale.

18. To correctly spell a major scale, all seven letters of the musical alphabet should be represented.

19. The four accidentals in an E major scale are **F♯, G♯, D♯,** and **C♯.**

20. There are two flats in the key of E♭ major.

21. **F, A♭,** and **C♭** make up an Fdim triad.

22. There are three flats in the key of G major.

23. **E♭, G,** and **A♯** make up an E♭ major triad.

24. The chord symbol for diminished is a little hollow circle.

25. The chord symbol for augmented is the minus sign (-).

26. A major triad has no chord symbol; only the root note is shown.

27. All triads must start from the root to actually be considered a chord.

28. The term "triad" may be substituted with the word "chord".

29. All triads contain a root, third, and fifth, except for augmented.

30. A Gdisoriented chord is composed of an alienated fifth, demented seventh and a suspicious third.

31. The three different chord qualities that are found in the chords of major scale (triad formula) are Major, Minor, and Diminished.

32. The three different chord qualities that are found in the chords of the minor scale (triad formula) are Major, Minor, and Diminished.

33. The v chord of the minor scale is sometimes altered as a V7 chord.

34. Fmin7, Gdim, and Dbmaj7 are found in the keys of Ab major and C minor.

35. Emaj7, D#dim, and Bmaj7 are found in the keys of E major and B major.

VII. Name each interval, triad, or seventh chord shown below.

VIII. Write each of the triads and seventh chords on the staff.

1. Ab7   2. Emaj7   3. C-7   4. B7   5. F#sus7   6. Gdim 7   7. C +   8. G-

9. Eb   10. A+   11. Esus   12. D-7   13. Bmin   14. Fmaj7   15. G7   16. B+(maj7)

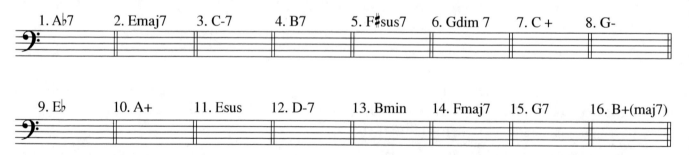

IX. Name the 7th chords of each scale below. Write each chord in each blank circle shown.

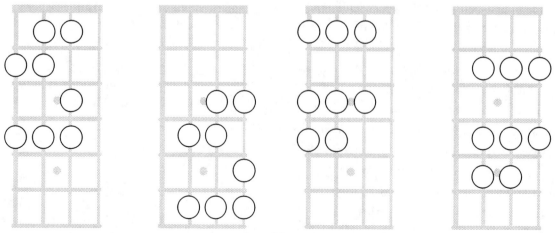

Chapter 1 Answers

Section I.

1. C
2. B♭
3. A♭
4. D
5. A
6. A♭, D♭, G♭, or C♭
7. A♭, D♭, G♭, or C♭
8. B
9. E
10. D

11. F
12. G♭
13. F♯
14. D♭
15. E♭, A♭, and B♭
16. B♭
17. D
18. major 2nd, major 3rd, major 6th, and major 7th
19. perfect fourth and perfect fifth
20. A, B, C♯, and D

Section II.

1. F   2. F   3. T   4. T   5. F   6. F   7. F   8. F   9. T   10. F

Section III.

1. C, D, E, F, G, A, and B
2. F, G, A, B♭, C, D, and E
3. B♭, C, D, E♭, F, G, and A
4. E♭, F, G, A♭, B♭, C, and D
5. A♭, B♭, C, D♭, E♭, F, and G
6. D♭, E♭, F, G♭, A♭, B♭, and C

7. G♭, A♭, B♭, C♭, D♭, E♭, and F
8. B, C♯, D♯, E, F♯, G♯, and A♯
9. E, F♯, G♯, A, B, C♯, and D♯
10. A, B, C♯, D, E, F♯, and G♯
11. D, E, F♯, G, A, B, and C♯
12. G, A, B, C, D, E, and F♯

Section IV is on the following page.

IV. The root of each scale is represented by a square.

C Major

F Major

B♭ Major

E♭ Major

A♭ Major

D♭ Major

G♭ Major

B Major

E Major

A Major

D Major

G Major

V.

VI.

1. A♭ major   2. C major   3. B♭ major   4. A major   5. G major   6. F major   7. E major   8. D major

Chapter 2 Answers

Section I.

1. A
2. F
3. C
4. G
5. F♯
6. E minor
7. C minor
8. F major
9. C♭ major
10. D♭ major
11. F
12. G minor
13. A♭ major
14. F minor
15. B♭, E♭, A♭
16. G minor
17. E
18. Major second
19. Perfect fourth, perfect fifth
20. minor third, minor sixth, and minor seventh.

Section II.

1. T   2. T   3. F   4. F   5. F   6. F   7. T   8. T   9. T   10. F

Section III.

1. C, D, E♭, F, G, A♭, and B♭
2. F, G, A♭, B♭, C, D♭, and E♭
3. B♭, C, D♭, E♭, F, G♭, and A♭
4. E♭, F, G♭, A♭, B♭, C♭, and D♭
5. G♯, A♯, B, C♯, D♯, E, and F♯
6. C♯, D♯, E, F♯, G♯, A, and B
7. F♯, G♯, A, B, C♯, D, and E
8. B, C♯, D, E, F♯, G, and A
9. E, F♯, G, A, B, C, and D
10. A, B, C, D, E, F, and G
11. D, E, F, G, A, B♭, and C
12. G, A, B♭, C, D, E♭, and F

See section IV is on the following page.

Section IV.

☐ = Root

C minor

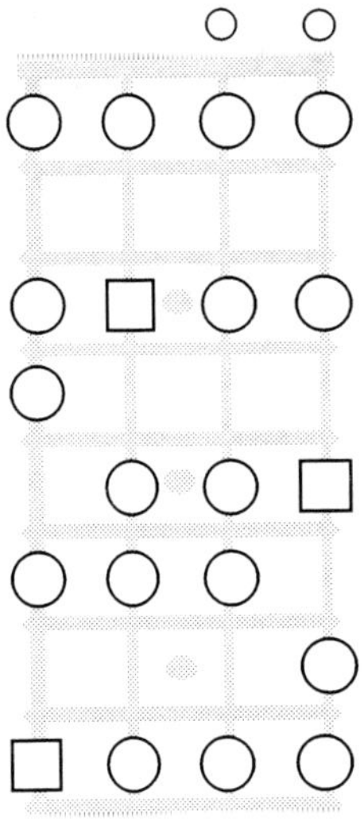

F minor

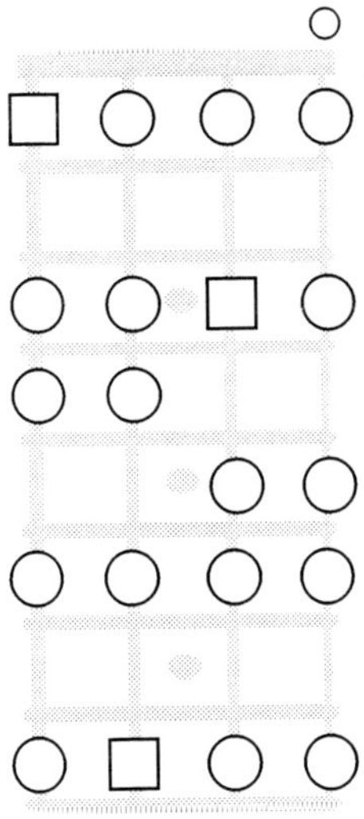

B♭ minor

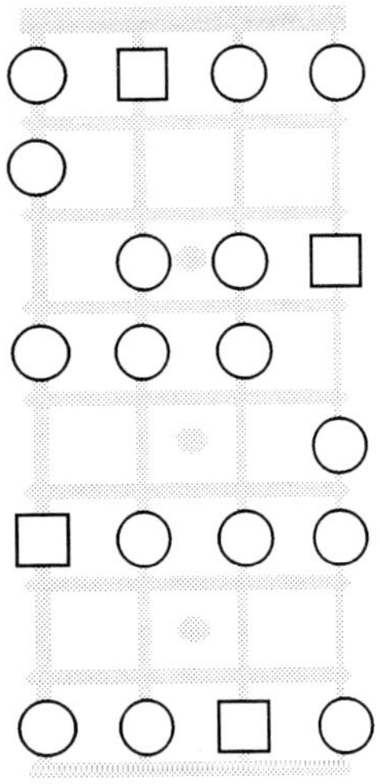

E♭ minor

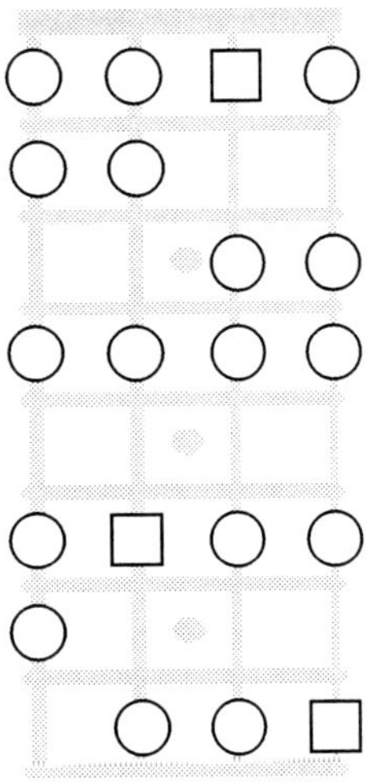

G♯ minor

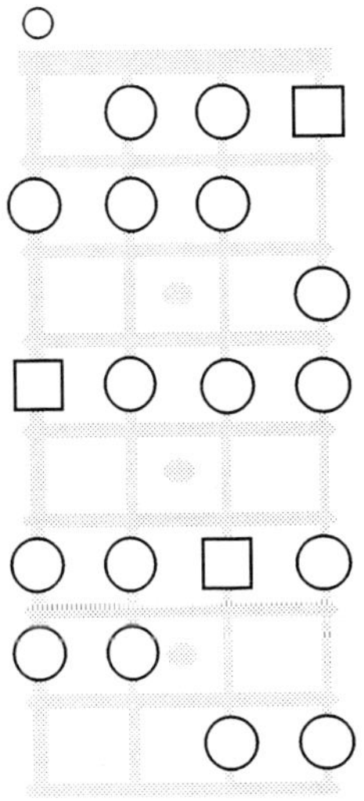

C♯ minor

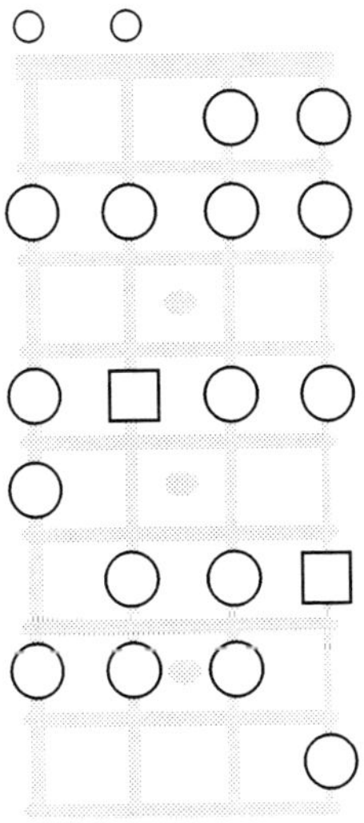

F♯ minor

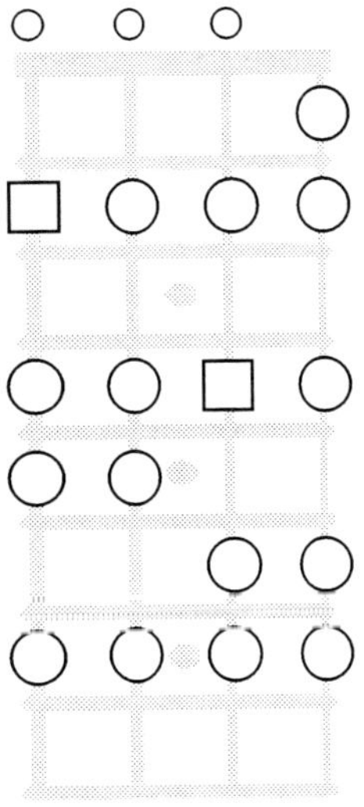

B minor

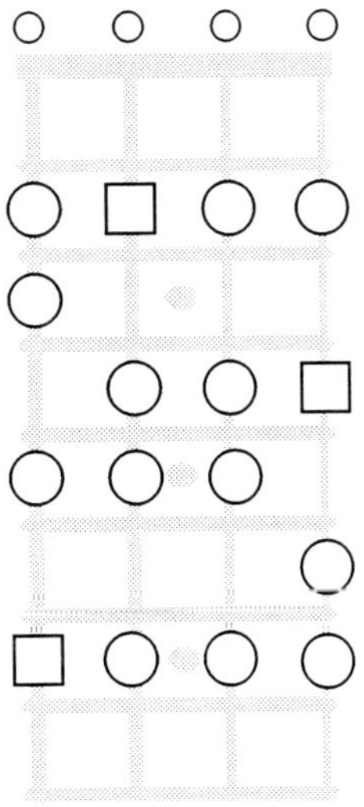

E minor

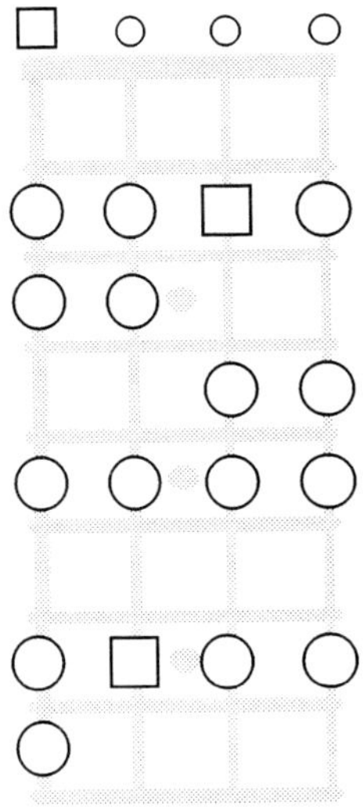

A minor

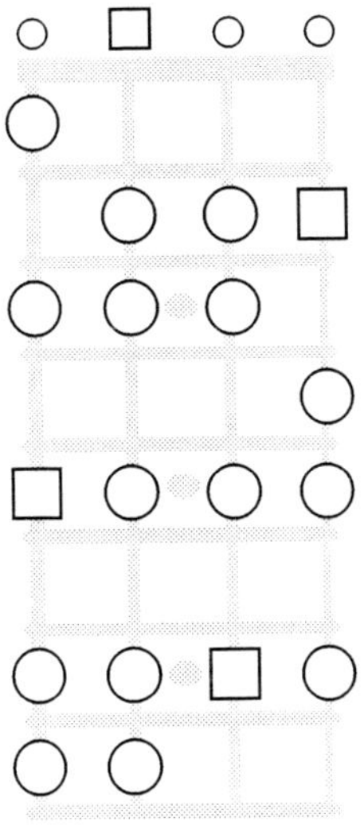

D minor

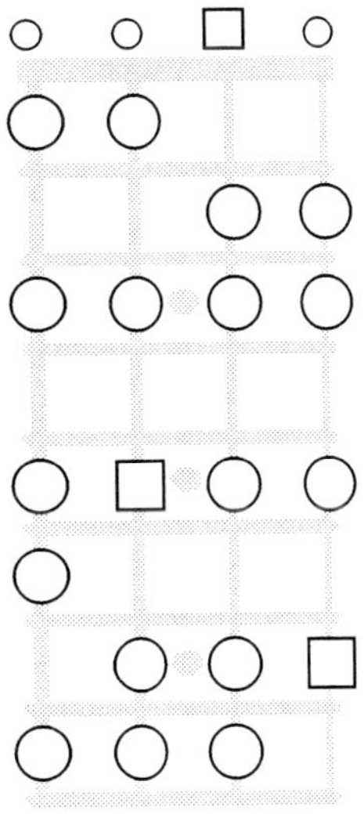

G minor

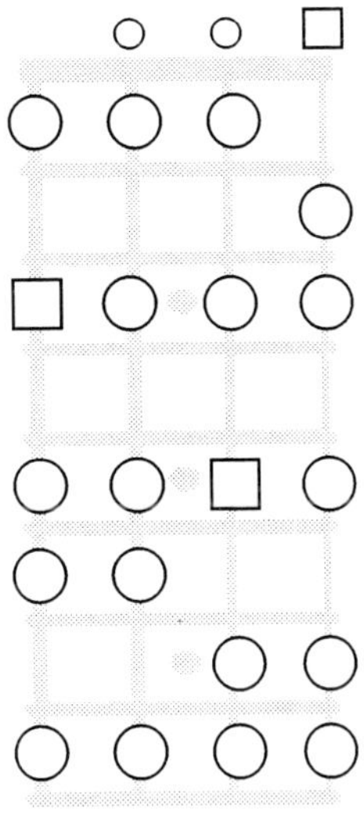

97

V.

VI.

1. F minor   2. D minor   3. E minor   4. G♯ minor   5. F♯ minor   6. A minor   7. B minor   8. C minor

Chapter 3 Answers

I.

1. Perfect 4th; C to F

2. Major 6th; C to A

3. Aug 4th, Dim 5th or tritone; C-F♯ or C-G♭

4. Aug 5th or Minor 6th; C-G♯ or C-A♭

5. Major 3rd; C-E

6. Major 2nd; C♯-D♯ or D♭-E♭

7. Major 6th; D-B

8. Major 3rd; E-G♯

9. Major 7th; G-F♯

10. Minor 7th; G♭-F♭ or F♯-E

11. Minor 2nd; C-D♭

12. Minor 2nd; A-B♭

13. Octave; B♭-B♭ or A♯-A♯

14. Minor 3rd; F♯-A

15. Major 2nd; G-A

16. Perfect 5th; E♭-B♭ or D♯-A♯

17. Minor 7th; A♭-G♭ or G♯-F♯

18. Aug 5th or Minor 6th; A-E♯ or A-F

19. Major 3rd; D-F♯

20. Minor 7th; B-A

21. Major 3rd; E-G♯

22. Major 3rd; F♯-A♯ or G♭-B♭

23. Minor 2nd; C-D♭

24. Tritone, Aug 4th or Dim 5th; F-B or F-C♭

25. Major 7th; G-F♯

26. Perfect 4th; D♭-G♭ or C♯-F♯

27. Major 2nd; B♭-C

II.

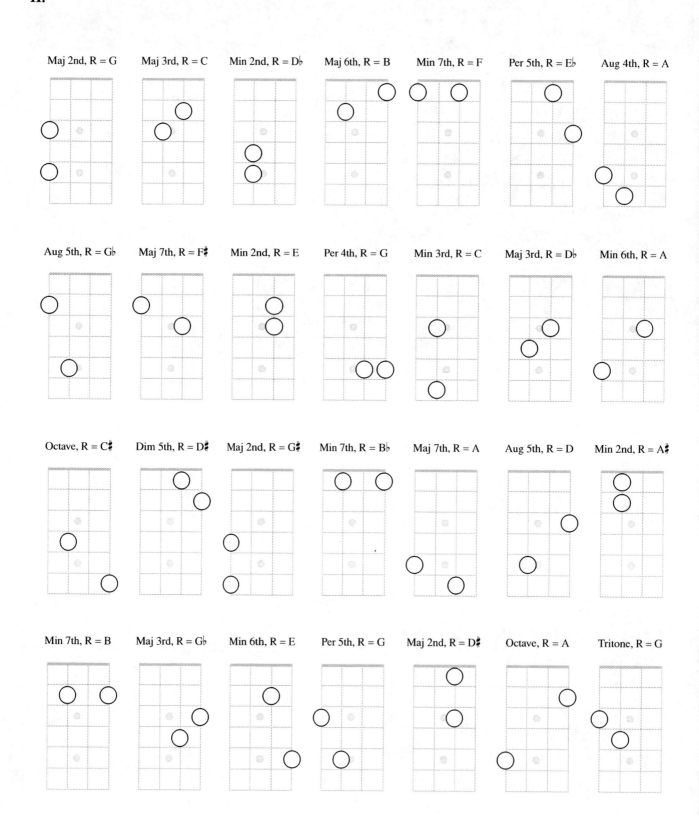

III.

1. B♭
2. G♯
3. C
4. B♭ or A♯
5. B♭
6. major 3rd
7. B♭
8. B
9. G♯
10. F

11. major third
12. A
13. D♯ or E♭
14. E
15. E
16. F♯
17. 2
18. 3
19. B♭
20. 6

IV.

1. Maj 2nd
2. Tritone or Dim 5th
3. Aug 4th or tritone
4. Min 2nd
5. Maj 6th
6. Octave
7. Maj 7th
8. Maj 3rd

9. Per 5th
10. Maj 7th
11. Maj 3rd
12. Maj 2nd
13. Tritone or Aug 4th
14. Per 4th
15. Tritone or Dim 5th
16. Aug 4th ot Tritone

V.

Chapter 4 Answers

I

1. Csus
2. Fm
3. Bm
4. A+
5. C
6. Gdim
7. D
8. E+
9. Gm
10. F#dim or Gbdim
11. Dsus
12. F#m or Gbm
13. G+
14. F#dim or Gbdim
15. F
16. Bm
17. Absus or G#sus
18. Bdim
19. F#+ or Gb+
20. Db or C#
21. Dbm or C#m
22. Bsus
23. E
24. G+
25. Dbdim or C#dim
26. Csus
27. Gm

II

Major, Root = A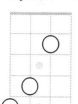

Minor, R = F

Aug, R = Bb

Major, R = B

Dim, R = G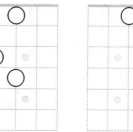

Sus, R = Eb

Major, R = D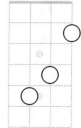

Minor, R = Gb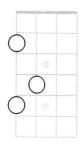

Dim, R = A#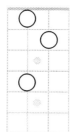

Aug, R = E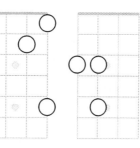

Sus, R = G

Major, R = F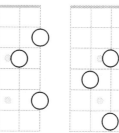

Major, R = Db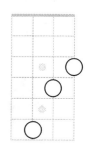

Minor, R = Eb

Dim, R = Db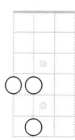

Sus, R = G#

Major, R = B

Aug, R = Bb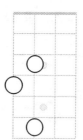

Major, R = Ab

Minor, R = A

Aug, R = F#

Minor, R = B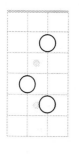

Aug, R = Eb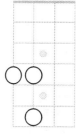

Dim, R = C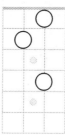

Major, R = G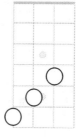

Sus, R = D#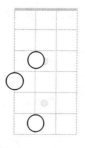

Minor, R = D

Major, R = G#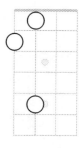

Minor, R = B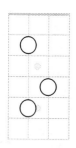

Aug, R = Eb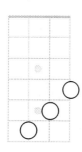

Dim, R = C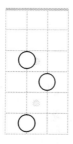

Major, R = G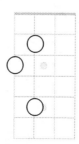

Sus, R = D#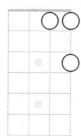

Minor, R = D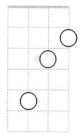

Major, R = G#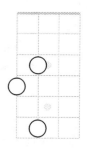

IV.

1. A+
2. D♭m
3. B♭
4. Gsus
5. Cm
6. Edim
7. F♯m
8. Ddim
9. Em
10. D+
11. Asus
12. F♯
13. E♭+
14. G+
15. Csus
16. A♭

IV.

1. Major 2. Minor 3. Aug 4. Dim 5. Sus 6. Dim 7. Major 8. Minor

9. Minor 10. Aug 11. Dim 12. Major 13. Minor 14. Sus 15. Dim 16. Major

V.

1. Cmajor
2. F, A, and C♯
3. Perfect 4th and Perfect 5th
4. Aminor
5. True
6. False
7. G, B♭, and D
8. Maj 3rd and Per 5th.
9. F♯Aug
10. major, minor, augmented, diminished, and suspended
11. False
12. True
13. True
14. True
15. False
16. B, E, and F♯
17. A♭, C♭, and E♭
18. Minor 3rd and Perfect 5th
19. (-), m, or min
20. True
21. False. C-E-G♯
22. False. D♭-F♭-A♭♭
23. True
24. False. A♭-D♭-E♭
25. True

I.

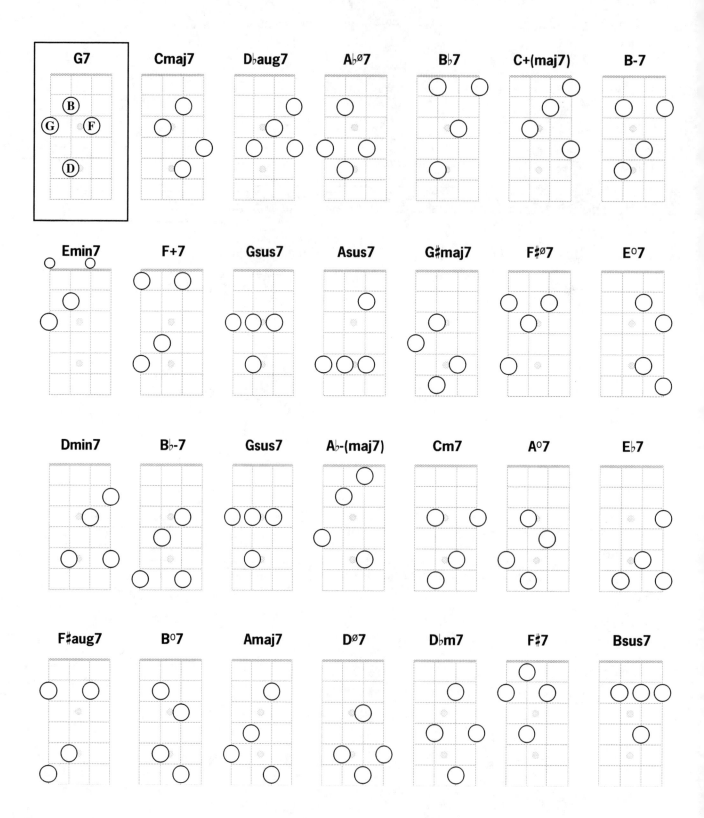

II.

1. F♯+7 or G♭+7
2. A+(Maj7)
3. G7
4. F♯sus7 or G♭sus7
5. B-7
6. B+(maj7)
7. E♭7
8. Gsus7
9. G♯maj7 or A♭maj7

10. C-7
11. A♯7 or B♭7
12. G-7
13. A♭dim7 or G♯dim7
14. Bmaj7
15. B♭7
16. B-7
17. F♯ half dim7
18. D+(maj7)

19. C half dim7
20. C♯sus7 or D♭sus7
21. G♯-7 or A♭-7
22. C7
23. A-(maj7)
24. E7
25. F+(maj7)
26. A♭ half dim7 or G♯ half dim7
27. Fsus7

III.

1. B7
2. A+7
3. Ddim7
4. G-7
5. E♭+(maj7)

6. G half dim7
7. A-7
8. Esus7
9. G+7
10. F♯-7

11. A half dim7
12. F♯7
13. B♭maj7
14. Bsus7
15. Fmaj7
16. Cdim7

IV.

1. Cmaj7   2. A♭+7   3. B-7   4. G7   5. A♭-7   6. Fdim7   7. Dmaj7   8. E♭7

9. B-(maj7)   10. F♯+7   11. Esus7   12. A7   13. B♭7   14. Gmin7   15. Em7   16. C+(maj7)

V.

1. T   2. T   3. F   4. T   5. T

VI.

1. D
2. D♭
3. B♭
4. F7
5. G

6. C♯°
7. G
8. G
9. B-7, Bm7, or Bmin7
10. major third, aug 5th, maj 7

Chapter 6 Answers

I.

1. B♭-
2. E♯dim
3. G
4. False
5. True
6. B♭maj7
7. Gmaj7
8. Cmaj7, A-7, Gmaj7
9. C-, F-, B♭, and E♭
10. E♭- and A♭
11. False (half-diminished)
12. True
13. True
14. True
15. True
16. False
17. major
18. diminished
19. D-, Fmaj7, G-7, and Edim
20. Amaj7

21. A♯-7 and D♯-7
22. Fmaj7
23. 5th
24. 7th
25. 7th
26. 2nd
27. False
28. False
29. True
30. False
31. True
32. True
33. C major
34. F minor
35. True
36. D-7, E♭maj7, F7, G-7, C-7, and B♭maj7
37. True
38. False
39. True
40. B-, G, and A

II.

1. A major = Amaj7, B-7, C♯-7, Dmaj7, E7, F♯-7, and G♯ half dim7
2. E♭ major = E♭maj7, F-7, G-7, A♭maj7, B♭7, C-7, and D half dim7
3. G minor = G-7, A half dim7, B♭maj7, C-7, D-7, E♭maj7, and F7
4. C minor = C-7, D half dim7, E♭maj7, F-7, G-7, A♭maj7, and B♭7

Final Review Answers

I.

1. Major 3rd, R=C
2. Maj 6th, R=A♭ or G♯
3. Maj 7th, R=B
4. Cdim
5. D♭7 or C♯7
6. D♭ fully dim7 or C♯ fully dim7
7. F♯ or G♭
8. Bdim
9. Maj 7th, root=F
10. D♯dim or E♭dim

11. G-(maj7)
12. Csus
13. Min 2nd, R=C
14. D+maj7
15. G♯ or A♭
16. tritone, dim 5th, or aug 4th, R=A♭ or G♯
17. D♯- or E♭-
18. Per 5th, R=B
19. G half dim7

20. C half dim7
21. C♯+ or D♭+
22. A♭dim or G♯dim
23. C
24. Min 6th or Aug 5th, R=F
25. C♯sus7 or D♭sus7
26. B-7
27. G♯7 or A♭7
28. Maj 3rd, R= G♯ or A♭

II.

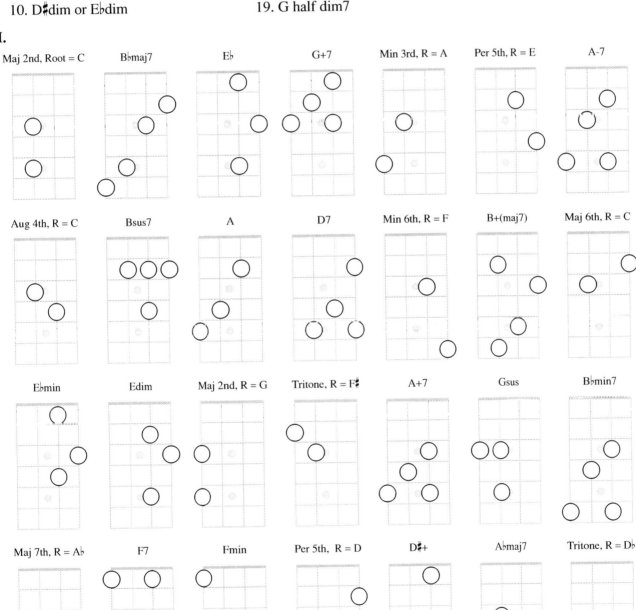

III.

1. G, A, B, C, D, E, and F♯
2. A♭, B♭, C, D♭, E♭, F, and G
3. B, C♯, D♯, E, F♯, G♯, and A♯
4. B♭, C, D, E♭, F, G, and A

5. A, B, C, D, E, F, and G
6. D, E, F, G, A, B♭, and C
7. G♯, A♯, B, C♯, D♯, E and F♯
8. F, G, A♭, B♭, C, D♭, and E♭

IV.

F major

E A D G

F B♭
E A
G C F B♭
A D G C
B♭
E A D
C F B♭

E♭ major

D G

F B♭ E♭ A♭
G C F B♭
A♭
D G C
B♭ E♭ A♭
D
C F B♭ E♭

G minor

A D G

F B♭ E♭
A
G C F B♭
A D G C
B♭ E♭
A D
C F B♭ E♭

B♭ minor

F B♭ E♭ A♭
G♭
C F B♭
A♭ D♭ G♭
C
B♭ E♭ A♭ D♭
C F B♭ E♭

V.

1. D
2. A
3. A
4. E♭
5. perfect 5th
6. E
7. G
8. F
9. C
10. G♯
11. 4 1/2
12. 2 1/2
13. D
14. E♭
15. G♯
16. G

17. D♭
18. F
19. A
20. C♯, F♯, and G♯.
21. D
22. maj 2nd, maj 3rd, maj 6th, and maj 7th
23. per 4th and per 5th
24. E minor
25. C minor
26. F
27. C♭
28. D♭ major
29. D♭
30. E
31. major second

32. per 4th and per 5th
33. C♯dim
34. A, C♯, and E♯
35. min 3rd and dim 5th
36. A+
37. F, A♭, and C
38. maj 3rd and per 5th
39. F♯ dim
40. major, minor, augmented, diminished, and suspended
41. D, G, and A
42. E, G♯, and B
43. minor third and perfect 5th
44. +
45. D
46. C♭

47. F
48. F♯7
49. A
50. E°7
51. D major
52. D minor
53. C-7, D♭maj7, E♭7, F-7, B♭-7, A♭maj7
54. C-, G-, B♭
55. A♭ major
56. D♯ minor
57. F-7, A♭maj7, B♭7, C-7, and E♭maj7
58. B-, E-, F♯m
59. B-7, Cmaj7, D7, E-7, A-7, Gmaj7
60. A-, F, E-

VI.

1. F 2. F 3. F 4. F 5. T 6. T 7. F 8. F 9. T 10. F 11. F 12. T
13. F 14. F 15. T 16. F 17. F 18. T 19. T 20. F 21. T 22. F 23. F 24. T
25. F 26. T 27. F 28. T 29. F 30. T 31. T 32. T 33. T 34. F 35. F

VII.

1. maj 3rd 2. maj 6th 3. dim 5th 4. octave 5. aug 5th 6. min 3rd 7. F- 8. Gsus
9. Edim 10. B 11. Cdim 12. Fmaj7 13. D+7 14. E7 15. Cmaj7 16. G- (ma7)

VIII.

1. Ab7 2. Emaj7 3. C-7 4. B7 5. F#sus7 6. Gdim7 7. C+ 8. G-

9. Eb 10. A+ 11. Esus 12. D-7 13. Bmin 14. Fmaj7 15. G7 16. B+(maj7)

IX.

1. F#maj7, G#min7, A#min7, Bmaj7, C#7, D#min7, E# half-dim7

2. Dbmaj7, Ebmin7, Fmin7, Gbmaj7, Ab7, Bbmin7, C half-dim7

3. Fmin7, G half-dim7, Abmaj7, Bbmin7, Cmin7, Dbmaj7, Eb7

4. Bmin7, C# half-dim7, Dmaj7, Emin7, F#min7, Gmaj7, A7

Glossary

Accidental – Indicates displacement of a note, symbolized by a sharp (♯) flat (♭), or natural (♮) sign.

Ascending scale – Climbing from the lowest note of a scale to the highest.

Augmented – 1. Name of a chord spelled with a root, major third, and a raised fifth. 2. To raise, or make larger. To expand.

Bar – Measure.

Bass clef— Clef in which the electric bass range is written. Electric bass sounds one octave lower than written.

Chord – Three or more notes played simultaneously. Types of chords include triads, 7th chords, 9th chords, 11th chords, and 13th chords.

Chord progression – When two or more chords are played in succession.

Chord-scale relationship – When a chord is extracted from a scale, or a scale is imposed over a chord. Ex. Cmaj7 is related to C Major because the intervals overlap each other.

Clef – Sign at the beginning of a staff to determine the pitch of notes.

Consonant – Intervals and chords that are resolute and blend together well.

Descending scale – Scale played from the highest note to the lowest.

Diatonic – Descriptive of the major scale, though it can also refer to minor scales as well.

Diminished— 1. Name of chord spelled with root, minor third, and flatted 5th. 2. Decreased in size; lowered.

Dissonant— Intervals and chords that clash or have a chaotic effect.

Dominant – Refers to a R-3-5-♭7 chord, minor seventh, or seventh chord built on the V.

Enharmonic – One note that can be called two different names. Ex. C♯ and D♭ are the same sounding note.

Fretboard – Bass or guitar fingerboard on which strings are depressed.

Flat – To lower a note by a fret or a half-step. Represented by the (♭) sign.

Half-diminished— Refers to a diminished seventh chord with a flat seventh (R-♭3-♭5-♭7).

Half step – A distance of one fret.

Harmony – Chord, scale, and interval structure that supports melody.

Interval – The distance between two notes.

Inversion – A triad or chord that begins with any other chord tone but the root.

Key – The tonal structure in which music is implied.

Key signature – Sharps and flats placed at the beginning of the staff that indicated tonal structure.

Measure – Bar.

Melody – A series of notes. Opposite of harmony.

Melodic interval – Occurs when the notes of an interval are sounded separately.

Octave – Two notes that have the same name, but are twice the frequency apart.

Position – Refers to the fretting-hand technique. Playing in a certain region of the bass neck.

Quality – Major, minor, augmented, suspended, or diminished. Descriptive of a scale, chord, or interval.

Roman Numeral formula – Series of chords generated by the major or minor scale, and represented by Roman numerals (I-ii-iii-IV-V-vi-vii).

Root – The fundamental note of an interval, triad, seventh chord or scale.

Root movement – The movement of changing in a musical piece. Specifically refers to the roots of these chords, and measuring them by their interval structure. Ex. Cmaj7 to Fmaj7. The root movement of C to F is a perfect fourth.

Scale – Series of notes.

Scale degree – Any note of a scale that is referenced by its interval structure, or Roman numeral.

Seventh chord – A four note chord with a root, third, fifth, and seventh of varying qualities.

Sharp – To raise a note by one fret. Described with the (♯) symbol.

Staff – Basis for standard music notation. Represented by five horizontal lines.

Suspended – One of the five basic groups of chords. Also refers to note tension that sounds unresolved.

Tab— Abbreviation for tablature.

Tablature – Graphical depiction of a bass or guitar fretboard.

Time signature – A sign at the beginning of the staff that indicates meter.

Tonality – Key. Refers to a series of notes that imply a scale or quality.

Tonic – The root of a scale or key.

Whole-step – Two frets distance on a bass neck.